Atha Westbury

**Australian Fairy Tales**

Atha Westbury

**Australian Fairy Tales**

ISBN/EAN: 9783743307148

Manufactured in Europe, USA, Canada, Australia, Japa

Cover: Foto ©ninafisch / pixelio.de

Manufactured and distributed by brebook publishing software (www.brebook.com)

Atha Westbury

**Australian Fairy Tales**

"The globe slowly split in twain." (Page 32.)

Australian Fairy Tales.] [Frontispiece

# CONTENTS.

GOLDEN CLOUD:—

|  |  | PAGE |
|---|---|---|
| CHAP. I. | THE LONE ROCK | 9 |
| " II. | MOTHER DOT | 19 |
| " III. | DUSK'S STRONGHOLD | 27 |
| " IV. | THE RING-DOVE | 34 |
| " V. | GOLDEN CLOUD | 42 |

TWILIGHT:—

| CHAP. I. | BARON THIMBLE | 48 |
|---|---|---|
| " II. | PRINCE PICNIC | 57 |
| " III. | LADY LOLLYPOP | 65 |

| TIM | . | 73 |
|---|---|---|
| THREE SPARROWS | . | 82 |
| KING DUNCE | . | 91 |
| "I DON'T KNOW" | . | 98 |
| THE BANK CAT | . | 106 |
| GUMTREE HOLLOW | . | 115 |

WHISKERKISS:—

| CHAP. I. | THE MYSTERIOUS JOURNEY | 123 |
|---|---|---|
| " II. | PRINCESS GOLDEN HAIR | 131 |

| A CROOKED SIXPENCE | . | 139 |
|---|---|---|
| THE BALL IN THE DELL | . | 148 |
| ELSIE | . | 155 |

## CONTENTS.

| | PAGE |
|---|---|
| THE WISHING-CAP | 162 |
| TWO GIANTS | 176 |
| MOTHLAND | 184 |
| MOONLAND | 197 |
| "SAILOR" | 221 |
| NELLIE | 228 |
| IN THE CLOUDS | 243 |
| WONDERLAND | 251 |
| BABY'S VISITORS | 259 |
| RUBYWINGS:— | |
|     CHAP. I. THE JOURNEY | 264 |
|     „ II. SHADOWS | 271 |
| LIFE AND DEATH | 277 |
| GIANTS | 283 |
| THE KANGAROO HUNTER:— | |
|     CHAP. I. THE LOST DRESS | 291 |
|     „ II. QUIZ | 298 |
|     „ III. A SLEEPING BEAUTY | 304 |
| THE LAUGHING JACKASS:— | |
|     CHAP. I. LOST IN THE BUSH | 312 |
|     „ II. EMU ROYAL | 319 |
| HOP-O'-MY-THUMB | 325 |
| A MAGIC WHISTLE | 334 |
| "COCKY":— | |
|     CHAP. I. THE MAGIC HUT | 342 |
|     „ II. BROWN EYES | 350 |

# LIST OF FULL-PAGE AND OTHER ILLUSTRATIONS.

"THE GLOBE SLOWLY SPLIT IN TWAIN" . . *Frontispiece*

|  | PAGE |
|---|---|
| "OUR HERO WENT SPRAWLING HEADLONG OVER HIM" . . | 20 |
| "AT THE SIGHT OF HER THE ASS BEGAN TO BRAY LOUDLY" . | 37 |
| "'SHAVE, OR HAIR CUT, SIR?' ASKED THE BARBER" . . | 51 |
| "A TALL, HANDSOME YOUNG MAN, ROBED IN A SUPERB HUNTING COSTUME" . . . . . | 71 |
| "GET UP, TOBY THE GROWLER, AND FOLLOW ME" . . | 83 |
| "SPEEDING AWAY ACROSS THE COUNTRY AS SWIFT AS THE WIND" . . . . . . . . . | 93 |
| "A JACK-IN-THE-BOX . . . CAME AND REVILED HIM" . . | 102 |
| "'HURRAH!' HE CRIED, TOSSING UP HIS HAT" . . . | 119 |
| "SEATED BENEATH A CANOPY OF ROSES" . . . . | 134 |
| "'PRAY TAKE OUT THOSE HORRID LONG SPIKES'" . . | 157 |
| "THE FAIRIES FLED IN GREAT HASTE" . . . . | 165 |
| "BOTH HE AND THE DOG WERE ENVELOPED IN A DEEP MIST" . . . . . . . . . | 180 |

## LIST OF ILLUSTRATIONS.

|  | PAGE |
|---|---|
| "HE WAS BORNE ALONG SO SWIFTLY THAT HE NEARLY LOST HIS SENSES" | 199 |
| "HE WAS NOT CERTAIN WHETHER THE MONSTER WAS LEAPING OR FLYING" | 209 |
| "'WHY, SURELY, *YOU'RE* NOT THE MAN IN THE MOON?'" | 219 |
| "THE LOVELY BEING TOOK NELLIE BY THE HAND" | 233 |
| "IT WAS A GRAND BALLOON" | 245 |
| "THE MONSTER ... ADVANCED WITH A LARGE STONE" | 255 |
| "THE OLD MAN BENT LOW BEFORE THE ICE MONARCH" | 266 |
| "'I AM QUEEN OF THE BUTTERFLIES,' SHE REPLIED" | 268 |
| "'WHAT KIND OF BIRD ARE YOU?'" | 295 |
| "'YOU CAN'T BE OUR JACK?'" | 315 |
| "'THOU ART VERY STRONG FOR SO SMALL A MAN'" | 329 |
| "ITS EYES WERE DREADFUL TO BEHOLD, AS IT CAME SLOWLY OUT OF THE WATER." | 352 |

# AUSTRALIAN FAIRY TALES.

## GOLDEN CLOUD.

*A CHRISTMAS STORY FOR YOUNG PEOPLE.*

### CHAPTER I.

#### THE LONE ROCK.

AUSTRALIA! Hast thou no enchanted castles within thy vast domain? Is there not one gallant youth, ready armed to do battle for the fair ones, sleeping 'neath the spell of wicked genii?

Come, youngsters, draw up your chairs. Come, mothers, ye who live your romantic girlhood o'er again in that of your children. Form up, gentlemen, fathers, hard men of the world, whose brows are wrinkled with care and worry, take rank in rear of your fair helpmates. Merchant, lock thy safe, close thy ledgers; horny-handed sons of toil, throw aside your implements of trade; gather near. I am going to draw aside the magic curtain which hides the great continent, marked on our map UNKNOWN. Turn down the lights—our magic lantern is quite ready. Hey presto! Look!

Why, what is this? The heart of a deep mine! A gold mine, with all its dim and rugged corridors, its tunnels and windings, lighted only by a dull taper here and there. There is no one at work, for it is Christmas Eve. Yet the underground region is not altogether untenanted. One man whose duty it is to watch the place, until relieved on the morrow, lies coiled up asleep in one of the long drives. He is a young man, not tall, but strongly made, and with limbs like another Hercules. On account of his great strength and a certain good temper combined, his mates call him, Samson the Nugget.

For what length of time the Nugget slumbered on this good Christmas Eve will never be known. Certain it is that he suddenly opened his eyes and beheld one of the biggest, and withal one of the ugliest, hulking fellows he had ever seen standing over him. The Nugget was a brave youth, but fear began to take possession of him as he looked at the intruder—a giant in stature, with a huge, flat head upon his shoulder, and a mouth as large, and about the shape of the newspaper receiver at the General Post Office. He carried a lamp in his hand, but there was a queer sheen from his eyes, which illumined the cavern with a fiery glow. His dress was a brown russet, his hat, sugar-loaf in shape, and he carried a sapling for a cudgel.

"Get up, Samson the Nugget, and follow me," said he in a brief, gruff tone.

"Who are you?" cried our hero, rising to his feet, and seizing a heavy iron drill.

"I am the strongest man in Golden Cloud, and my name is Grapple," rejoined the other grimly. "Will you come?"

"Where?" said the Nugget. "There is no way out of this mine except by the cage up the shaft."

"That's all you know about it," returned Grapple, with a grim laugh. "If I find a way, have you courage to follow?"

The Nugget felt inclined to refuse point blank, but curiosity being strong within him, he bowed an assent.

Grapple, without a word, turned on his heel and led the way further down the dark recesses of the tunnel. Our hero followed. Of one thing the miner felt certain—that the end of the drive would effectually bar the progress of his unwelcome visitor. Strange to relate, such was not the case.

The narrow passage appeared to extend and widen out before their advance, until it took the shape of a long railway tunnel, from which the pair emerged at length into the bright beams of day. The transit from what seemed to be the bowels of a high mountain range to a landscape fairer and more beautiful than our hero had ever seen, filled his mind with wonder. His companion, now that daylight was upon him, did not seem such an ugly customer after all. He was certainly a huge, grotesque-looking personage, but there wasn't a bit of malice in anything he said or did.

Our hero's amazement was so great, that it was some considerable time before he found words wherewith to address his companion.

"What country is this?" he asked, turning to Grapple.

"This is Golden Cloud."

"Golden Cloud! I never heard of such a place. Why did you bring me here?"

"Because I wanted a companion on my travels," rejoined the other. "I heard you were a very strong man, and I determined to fetch you out of that dismal mine, so that you might enjoy your Christmas holidays with me."

"Oh, indeed! very considerate on your part, my friend, but what if I return to the mine?" said the Nugget.

"You can't—not without my aid," responded Grapple. "Now don't be a fool. I'm going on a sort of excursion into the interior, and I want a companion. We shall not be long away, and I promise to lead you safely back to the place from whence you came as soon as we return."

The Nugget reflected. He felt a strong desire to see something of this most charming country. Besides, he saw that this strange creature had uttered the truth. He could not possibly find his way back to the mine alone.

Here it must be remarked that, although our hero was only a miner, he possessed both intelligence and culture, not usually found in men of his class. He had read much, and had a longing for the romantic, and in short, in less time than it takes to write this sentence, Samson the Nugget had resolved to go on a holiday tour with his quaint companion.

It is needless to describe their journey for the first two days; suffice it that the route lay through the tangled maze of a pathless forest of noble trees, where branches intertwining overhead formed a leafy canopy for many miles. On the third day

Grapple and his companion emerged upon a wide, extensive plain. Towering in the distance, like a pyramid, they observed a gigantic rock standing out above the level expanse around. The sun, gleaming upon its peaks and spires, gave it a weird, fantastic look, as if some great magician of the olden time had bade it rise with the lifting of his wand. As far as the vision reached along the line of the horizon, the plain seemed ringed in by the magnificent bush-land through which they had come. Nearer, however, there was a broad river flowing its slow way round the lone cliff; the sheen of its waves forming a massive girdle, which flashed back the sun's rays a thousandfold.

The evening was drawing nigh as the Nugget and Grapple approached the lofty crag, and they determined to pass the night beneath its sheltering base. For this purpose they crossed a ford on the river, and ascended a wide slope of rich, green sward, softer than velvet, and entered an enclosed space, which had evidently been a most lovely garden at one time. To the gaze of our hero it appeared nothing but a mass of weeds and ragged, bare shrubs, under which a whole multitude of kangaroos, emus, wallabies, wild goats, and native bears were gathered in wild confusion.

The Nugget was filled with amazement as he beheld these animals. Their number was countless, and the tameness with which they submitted to be fondled was more extraordinary still. Indeed, they never moved as the two men strode through their ranks, no more than if they had been so many posts wanting life and movement. The astonishment of our hero was in no way diminished as they reached the western face of the supposed rock. Here they saw a broad flight of steps leading towards a ponderous gateway. The gate stood wide open, and on either side, mounted on pillars of granite, were the carved figures of two gigantic black fellows, each leaning on a spear. Grapple and his companion entered the portal, and found themselves in a lofty corridor, supported by massive columns of polished masonry. To the right and left of them, as they advanced, splendid apartments, vast in their dimensions, and upholstered with costly furniture, met their gaze. It was not the magnitude of the place, nor the fine things therein, which filled them with such speechless amazement, but the wonderful statuary they saw. These figures were in every room, and were so life-like in their dimensions and appearance, that the Nugget was fain to believe that they were flesh and blood. Ladies and gentlemen were represented quite naturally, and in various places and functions. Yonder a group were seated round the banquet in the act of eating. There another group, mostly ladies, gossipping and laughing. Some had been chiselled walking, some kneeling, others kissing, many reading. The same view met the travellers from one end of this strange mansion to the other. Nothing could seem more substantial, more real, than these beautiful models, attired as they were in robes of gorgeous hue and texture, but foreign and altogether unfamiliar to our hero, who often touched them with his hand. Twenty times he addressed them, but not one answered. They were only images, nothing more. Body, limbs, robes—all were cold and hard as stone to the touch.

Their curiosity appeased, our hero and his companion selected a small but comfortable apartment wherein to pass the night. They had killed a kangaroo the previous day, from the remains of which they dined; then they retired, and both were soon fast asleep.

The Nugget had scarcely closed his eyes, however, ere he was roused by the application of a hard whack on the drum of his left ear.

Now it chanced that Grapple lay on that side of the Nugget and judging hastily, as people are apt to do under similar conditions, our hero sprang up, and began to pound his bedfellow soundly.

"Hold! stop! What is this all about?" cried poor Grapple.

"Did you not give me a blow?" demanded the Nugget fiercely.

"I? Certainly not."

"Oh, indeed! I suppose the man in the moon did it. There are only two of us here, sir," cried the Nugget.

"I'll swear I did not do it. Your blows awakened me."

"Humph! It is very strange," cried they, and they grumbled at each other until they fell asleep again.

Not long did the pair enjoy repose. This time Grapple started up with a yell of agony.

"Coward!" he cried, and without further warning he fell upon the Nugget and tried to choke him. We have said that Samson was a powerful fellow. Exerting the full force of his muscles, he overpowered his adversary, and briefly demanded an explanation.

"Wretched, false friend! what have I done that you should stab me with your knife?" cried Grapple, with a groan.

The young miner burst out in a hearty guffaw.

"Look here, my friend," he replied quickly, "I think both of us have been the dupes of some rascally enemies hereabout. I receive a thump on the ear, you a wound in the leg, when both of us are sound asleep. Mum! Let us to slumber again. Daylight will be here anon; in the meantime, I will keep watch to discover our lurking foe."

Grapple assented. Having bound up his leg the travellers lay down again as if nothing had happened.

The Nugget, however, slept like a cat, otherwise he would not have seen the most withered, and, at the same time, most repulsive-looking individual in the world stealing noiselessly out on tip-toe from behind one of the statues in the corridor. The day was breaking, and every object could be clearly distinguished. Watching the intruder, our hero saw he was a dwarf, and a very ugly one. The body of the wee monster was like an ale keg, from which protruded short, sturdy limbs. His hands were dreadfully large, the skin knobbed and gnarled like the bark of a tree. A head, the counterpart of a Christmas pudding with a slice cut out for a mouth, a parsnip for a nose, and a pair of agates for eyes, and you have a rough photograph of the wretch that now advanced as stealthily as a shadow toward our hero and his companion.

As he drew near the prostrate pair he stooped over the Nugget to inflict a blow on his head. Our hero bounded up and tried to catch his foe. Vain effort. With the agility and quickness of a professional wrestler, the dwarf upset the astonished digger as if he had been no more than a schoolboy; then, fleeing along the corridor, he cleared the steps of the gate at one bound and ran swiftly across the garden towards the river.

## CHAPTER II.

### MOTHER DOT.

SAMSON the Nugget was taken "all aback," as the sailors say, at the unexpected attack of his wee but nimble opponent. Yet, before the dwarf had time to reach the garden wall, our hero was up and pursued his foe. Like a kangaroo when the hunters are in full cry, the little man bounded down the slope leading to the river, over the stream, and away across the open space, with prodigious leaps rather than with the stride of a runner. Tally-ho! A stern chase is a long chase, but in this case the adage could not be applied, inasmuch as our hero was sound in wind and limb, and, moreover, he was a sturdy pedestrian.

He soon gained upon his antagonist, when the latter, ready and fertile in devices, adopted tactics which gave him an advantage, and enabled him

"OUR HERO WENT SPRAWLING HEADLONG OVER HIM."

to over-reach his pursuer. They were on the edge of the bushland which bordered the plain, and the dwarf, slacking speed, suffered Samson to approach within arm's length, when, turning suddenly, he cast himself flat down, whereupon our hero went sprawling headlong over him. Laughing triumphantly, the dwarf sprang to his feet, and jumped off again in the cover of the bush.

As the miner recovered himself and resumed the pursuit, he observed the chase unexpectedly disappear from view behind a tuft of coarse grass and weeds growing at the base of a gigantic bloodtree. Thinking the antic sprite was forming another trap, the young miner approached the spot cautiously. It was lucky he did so, for in parting the rubbish aside he discovered a wide, deep hole, about the dimensions of an ordinary well. There were neither steps nor ladder down this gaping pit, whose bottom lay far beneath the ken of Samson the Nugget, who stood gazing down the dim void, wondering if the little monster had vanished down it by some potent agency only known to himself. Watching and waiting, Samson satisfied himself that the dwarf had certainly gone down the hole, and he determined to follow him.

With this object in view, our hero marked the spot and retraced his way to the rock. Grapple still slept soundly. Not wishing to disturb him, the Nugget proceeded to the rear of the premises, where he found a long stout rope. With it he returned to the well. Having securely fastened one end of the rope to the tree, he threw the remainder down the chasm, and then began to descend hand over hand. It cannot be denied that this was a dangerous undertaking, but the Nugget, being a digger, and not lacking in pluck, the cost was not considered. From the first moment our hero had set eyes on the little monster it had somehow come to him that the sprite was in some mysterious manner connected with all the ruin and wreck he had seen at the rock.

Clinging firmly to the rope, the Nugget descended until he reached the end of it. Looking far down he beheld the same dark void, apparently bottomless. While he swayed to and fro like a toy at the end of a string, his pendant body thumped against something that sounded dull and hollow, and he saw he had burst open a secret door in the wall. Planting his foot firmly on the threshold of the aperture, the adventurer let go the rope and found himself in a low, arched cavern. The extremity brought him face to face with a bright landscape, varying both in hue and shade from the region he had just quitted. Right before him a tiny cascade of pure spring water spurted from the breast of the cliff on which he stood, and meandered its course through a belt of trees so quiet and silent that our hero felt appalled at its stillness. There was a broad, well-worn pathway down into the dell, and the Nugget made his way thither. As he walked smartly along, looking right and left of him, he espied a very ancient dame seated upon a bundle of firewood she had evidently gathered. By her side were two large baskets of wild fruit.

"Good-morrow, ma'am," cried the miner, courteously lifting his hat. "Pray have you seen a very ugly little man pass this way?"

"My son, all men are lovely in my eyes," replied the crone, and she looked at him with eyes that gleamed like the orbs of a cat in the darkness. "Do you know, I'm right glad you came this way. You look strong. Will you carry my parcels for me?"

"Certainly I will," replied the Nugget cheerfully. "Where do you live?"

"My hut stands on the range yonder, on the other side of this bush. Dear me, how tired I am to be sure!"

How her cat's eyes glowed as she looked at him! The Nugget did not see nor heed anything about the old woman; his whole thoughts were centred on the capture of his foe.

"Come, madam," said he, "one good turn deserves another. Tell me where I may find the fellow I seek, and I'll carry your goods and yourself on top of them."

"Oh, good youth, haste is a bad master. If you seek for Dusk in haste, you'll never find him."

"Dusk! Who's Dusk, mother?"

"The dwarf you came to find," she answered quickly. "Beware, he's a cunning sprite."

The Nugget laughed. "I should only like the opportunity to measure weapons with the cowardly little imp," he said. "Have you seen him?"

"Yes; he passed this way not an hour ago," she answered.

"Thank you, dame. I'm off!" exclaimed our hero, hastily preparing to follow.

"Nay, good sir, you promised to carry my things," responded the dame.

"Bother your things! I'll return and carry them when I've caught Mr. Dusk."

"You will have trouble for nothing if you try it," she replied, her eyes glowing like coals of fire. "Fulfil your promise to me and I will help you."

"Agreed," cried our hero. "Make haste, good dame. Place the sticks upon my back and the baskets on my arms. That's it. Now come along."

Samson the Nugget, strong and powerful as he undoubtedly was, pulled a wry face as the load was put upon his person. The bundle of firewood seemed as heavy to him as so many bars of solid gold, while the baskets appeared to have been suddenly freighted with ingots of lead, the weight of which almost took away his breath. Nevertheless, our hero, nothing daunted, made an effort, and proceeded onward with his burden. Now, so long as the Nugget trod on level ground he managed pretty well, but when he came to the range and began its ascent, with the loose stones rolling from under his feet at every step, the man's immense muscular strength began to fail. Drops of perspiration stood upon his face and ran down his back, now hot, now cold.

"My good woman!" he cried, "I can go no farther till I have rested."

"Rested!" repeated the hag in scornful accents. "Hear the boaster. This is the man in search of Dusk, the strong. Hear him! He would attack the all-powerful genii; and yet, forsooth, he cannot carry what an old woman like me has so often borne up hill and down dale. Faugh!"

The Nugget put up his back like a vicious mule, and attempted to get rid of his load; but the sticks and the baskets clung to him as if these articles had grown there.

"Will you go on, sir?" cried the crone, with a mocking laugh.

The Nugget answered not; but with a vigorous effort tried to rid himself of the encumbrance. Vain task; his efforts only wearied him. Moreover, the hag made matters worse by jumping up upon the bundle of sticks; and though lean and withered as she certainly appeared, our hero felt her additional weight to be more than that of the stoutest wench of his acquaintance. To kick against the pricks was useless. So Samson, like a wise fellow, staggered on as he best could to the end of his journey. Arrived at the hut, the dame became kindness itself. She placed food and drink of the choicest kind before him, and when he had refreshed himself, said,—

"Young man, your task has been a severe one, but the reward I shall bestow will be all the greater on that account. For over twenty years no one has ever been found who could carry my parcels for me until to-day."

"I don't care to go shopping with you again in a hurry," muttered the Nugget, stretching out his tired limbs.

"I have neither money nor property to give you," she continued; "but my gift shall be more valuable to you than both combined. Behold! This is the horn of an enchanted ram. The animal was bred by my great grandsire, the King of

Moonshine, and the relic has been handed down to me. Take it, my son, and let me caution you to use its wonderful power wisely. With that in your possession, Dusk, the griffin, cannot escape you. For whatever you may wish for this relic shall supply."

With these words Mother Dot placed in the young man's hand a small, curled horn, highly polished, and on which were engraven three figures, and some words, in a language he did not understand, written beneath them. The Nugget thanked the old lady for her gift, and having sufficiently refreshed and rested himself, he set forward in search of Dusk, the dwarf.

## CHAPTER III.

### DUSK'S STRONGHOLD.

To say that our hero felt satisfied with the treatment he had received at the hands of Mother Dot would be to state an untruth. He was *not* satisfied. He had a latent suspicion that the hag was in some way or other leagued with his enemy. Under these circumstances he therefore thrust her gift into his pocket, and went in search of the ugly dwarf. For hours he wandered about without seeing a vestige of any living thing. He began to feel tired and hungry, and darkness was approaching fast. What should he do? Try and find his way back again to where he had left Grapple? No, the giant would only laugh at him.

He suddenly bethought him to try the old woman's gift. She had said that whatever he might wish for should be gratified. His first and dearest wish was to find the whereabouts of the dwarf. So he put the relic to the test. Swift and potent indeed was the effect. Scarcely had the desire taken shape in his mind ere his eyes beheld a massive structure about the distance of a mile right ahead of him. The building was surrounded by a high wall, and looked more like a gaol than anything else.

As he drew near, the young miner observed a strong iron door in the wall, at which he began to knock.

"Who's there? What want you here?" resounded from a hoarse voice belonging to an enormous head and face, which at that moment protruded itself over the battlement.

"Does the dwarf they call Dusk reside here?" demanded our hero.

"He does, but he's not at home. Go away, you mite, before I come and crush your bones together."

"Try," responded the Nugget. "As for the dwarf, I believe the rascal is here, and I mean to enter and satisfy myself on that point."

"Begone, you wretched ant—you insect!" roared the monster passionately.

"A fig for your bluster, you bundle of ugliness," responded our hero.

The face disappeared as suddenly as the policeman in the puppet show, and immediately the iron door opened wide, disclosing a horrible-looking fellow, several feet taller than Grapple, and armed with a well-seasoned sapling about the dimensions of a verandah post.

"Now, you flea, you miserable son-in-law of a blow-fly, what have you to say before I smash you up?" cried the giant, purple with rage.

Without answer, Samson sprang through the open doorway. As he did so, the monster aimed a crushing blow at his head. Ducking like an otter, Nugget avoided the ponderous bludgeon, which fell upon the door and tore it from its hinges. Quick as the swoop of a hawk, he seized a fragment of iron and dealt his gigantic antagonist an awkward whack full upon his stomach, which tumbled him down, as if he had been shot, and there he lay quite helpless.

The Nugget, without troubling about his adversary, entered the building; but he had not advanced beyond the porch before another and more formidable foe confronted him. Strongly built, and as sturdy as the trunk of an old oak, monster number two appeared neither man nor fish, but a strange combination of both. It had eyes and mouth like a fish, and as many legs and arms as an octopus, each member being armed at the extremities with spikes as sharp as steel.

"What seekest thou?" it bellowed forth, with the lungs of a bull.

"I seek the antic sprite, Dusk," replied the undaunted Samson.

"Poor, mean earthworm, knowest thou not that the mighty Dusk is lord and master here in Twilight?"

"Pray conduct me to his lordship."

"Hence! at once, or I'll roast you like a crab," said the man-fish.

"Stuff! You'll find me tough eating," replied the Nugget, at the same time drawing forth the ram's horn, and changing it into a light, handy sword.

The monster grinned in disdain. Stretching forth his long arms, he tried to clutch our hero, but the Nugget cleverly avoided him. Then began a fierce combat between them. Here and there, up and down, with ringing blows, the duel became very exciting and sanguinary, till the man-fish, losing his temper and his breath together, received the *coup de grâce*, and was hurled headlong down the terrace steps.

All further opposition seemed at an end with the death of the second monster, and our hero wended his way into the interior of the mansion. As he proceeded, he found the place was not at all so gloomy as might be expected from an outside view of it. Indeed, he discovered it was a large building, and furnished in excellent taste. The walls of the various apartments were hung with silk and velvet of chaste pattern and hue. Couches and chairs richly carved, with marble tables decked with choicest flowers and fruits, were reflected in mirrors on the walls, which were more elaborate than those of old Venice. Parrots of the gayest plumage, rare birds in golden cages, soft, sparkling fountains, and a delicious perfume of flowers, all made up a magnificent whole that was worthy the dwelling-place of a king.

With hasty steps our hero wandered through many rooms, hoping to discover the dwarf. His wandering brought him to a grand staircase, the steps of which were covered with Cashmere velvet, bordered with satin flowers. A bronze stand, curiously ornamented, supported a large globe of white crystal at the head of the stairway. The Nugget could not help pausing to admire this beautiful piece of workmanship. The crystal ball was so dazzling bright that it made his eyes ache to look upon it.

"What a strange ball!" he said, shading his sight with his hand, and approaching close to it. "How large it is! It seems large enough to hold that rascal Dusk. What if he should be hiding here? Perhaps it is solid. Humph! I'll try it. Ball, crystal ball, if thou art hollow, by my ram's horn, I command thee! Open!"

Before the words had left his lips the globe slowly split in twain; while from within there rose before his wondering sight—not the ugly sprite—but the graceful form of a lovely young maiden.

Never in the life of this poor digger, either in his waking sense or in dreams, had he seen any woman so enchantingly lovely. In olden times men were blessed with visions of the angels, and they essayed to picture what they had seen. Yet how crude the forms of Cherubim and Seraphim both on canvas and on page to the glorious reality!

If Samson the Nugget had been gifted with the descriptive powers of the world-renowned war correspondent, I'm afraid the twenty-six letters in our alphabet would not have been sufficient to convey any idea of the beauty of this damsel upon whom he gazed. Her complexion was like that delicate tint we see upon the pearl shell, and her hair shone like burnished gold.

"Who art thou, fair lady?" cried the Australian youth, gallantly advancing with outstretched hands to assist her from the pedestal whereon she had been imprisoned.

"Alas!" she answered, weeping, "I am the daughter of King Golden Cloud, and my name is Silverhaze. Because I would not consent to become the wife of a wicked dwarf, named Dusk, he stole me from my home, and conveying me here, enclosed me in yon crystal globe."

No ring-dove cooing for its mate had softer, sweeter voice than Princess Silverhaze. Our hero led her down the stairway and placed her on a couch by the window. Seating himself at her feet he briefly explained to her the part he had taken in search of their common foe.

"Where is Golden Cloud, your home?" he said. "I swear I will not rest until I have placed you safe again in the arms of your kith and kin."

"Thou art a brave youth," answered the Princess, looking down at him with eyes that sparkled gratitude. "If thou canst indeed take me from this horrid place, my father will load thee with honours, and poor Silverhaze will love thee always."

Ah me! Who shall write the Nugget's answer? Who shall detail his confusion, his stammerings, his schoolboy blushes? Not I, my young friends. Wise old Atha knows full well how near the Love God dangles to yourselves—how near ye are to the reality without the ideal being stamped on this page to point the way.

In considerably less time than it takes to pen these lines, the Princess had decided to trust her fortunes to the pluck and gallantry of her young champion. But in the midst of their plans they were unexpectedly confronted by their deadly enemy—Dusk—armed to the teeth.

## CHAPTER IV.

### THE RING-DOVE.

FAIRYLAND can produce nothing so wonderful as the facility with which sundry mortals can extend their faces. To smile widely is the fashion with us nowadays, and it is very wonderful indeed to note the various methods of its accomplishment. If the human face be a mask (and who shall say it is not?) then what maskers promenade our streets with their masks set smiling—as one would set a watch or a clock! Bowing and smirking is the latest humbug, and even the mere soulless puppets, born of men's brains, must smack of it, else they are voted untrue to life and nature.

There was a set smile on the ugly face of Dusk, the dwarf, as he bowed to Silverhaze and our hero; but the sprite had not been educated in a mortal school. He lacked polish. Malignity shone in his eyes and in every corner of his wicked mouth.

"Don't move, I pray," he said slowly; "my slaves are entirely at your service. Why don't you summon them to do your bidding? Ho, ho, ho!" And his mocking laugh rang through the vaulted pasages like a bugle-call.

Poor Silverhaze began to tremble, and clung to the Nugget for support, while the youth in his turn tried his utmost to calm her fears.

The dwarf eyed them with a sinister look. "Very charming for my fay," he ejaculated, rubbing his bony hands together. "Very loving and tender, oh, my doves. What tender morsels you'll make for mince-pies! My cook, Pancake Parecheese, will be delighted with you. He, he, hi!" He turned about as he spoke, and clapped his hands together as a signal. Almost immediately the room became filled with armed monsters.

"Ha!" cried Dusk in mocking sarcasm. "You break into my house, kill my servants, and rob me of my coveted prize. Slaves, take this man away and boil him down."

It was a dreadful order. To cook a man like a leg of mutton or a shin of beef! Good heavens! it was awful. But the dwarf, powerful as he was, little dreamed of the amazing influence of the ram's horn. By its potent force our hero set the whole army of monsters by the ears, who fell foul of and slew each other. Not satisfied with this, they set fire to the mansion, where, amidst the conflagration, those who were not slain perished in the flames.

At the beginning of the fray our hero seized the dwarf, and transforming him into a donkey, placed the King's daughter on his back, and retraced his steps to Mother Dot's hut on the cliff. The dame came out at their approach, and at the sight of her the ass began to bray loudly.

"Thou wicked sprite!" she cried, shaking her staff over him. "Thou camest to me in sore need, and I gave thee power. How hast thou used my gift? Why, to evil. Beast thou art, and a beast thou shalt remain for evermore."

The donkey drew back his long ears, and kicked spitefully, for fully five minutes, at the decree. Meanwhile, Mother Dot took the young Princess and her companion into the hut, and placed refreshment before them. It was amusing to see the attention the Nugget bestowed upon the fair young creature by his side, and to note the

"AT THE SIGHT OF HER THE ASS BEGAN TO BRAY LOUDLY."

tell-tale blushes which ever and anon suffused her face as their eyes or their hands chanced to meet. Even the old crone, who wasn't looking their way, nodded her ancient head, muttered, and chuckled in a wise way, as if she had known it all beforehand.

The meal ended, Silverhaze approached the dame and whispered, "Dear Mother Dot, who is this gallant youth who has delivered me from the wicked dwarf?"

"Ah, he will tell you soon, my pearl," she answered with a leer; "meantime, he's called the Knight of the Ram's Horn."

Presently the Nugget drew near the old woman, and plucking her by the sleeve, said, "Dame, canst tell what I am to do with this gentle maiden?"

"Yes, my son. Thou hast conquered the evil Dusk, therefore to thee shall be the proud service of restoring Princess Silverhaze to her home."

"Where is her home, good dame?"

"Thou hast seen it," answered the old woman. "That rock on the plain is the palace of King Golden Cloud. This damsel is the King's only child."

"Whew!" cried Samson, taking off his hat. "Why, mother, the place is a wretched ruin."

"So it is, and there stands the spoiler," replied the crone, pointing to the ass. "Dusk the dwarf coveted the Pearl of Golden Cloud for his wife, and when she denied him, the base wretch stole her from thence, and to hide the deed, he committed a greater one, as people generally do who begin to do evil. By the dwarf's enchantments, the King, Queen, ladies, nobles, courtiers, and every soul within the palace were transformed into the likeness of stone images. The guards who attempted to rescue the King's daughter were changed into a horde of wild animals on the spot, while the matchless garden, the wonder and beauty of a kingdom, became a wide waste."

"What a wicked monster!" cried our hero indignantly.

"Ah! my son, but thanks to thy strong back and unfaltering courage the spell is broken, and his power is gone for ever. If thou hadst failed with the burden I gave thee, then would Silverhaze be still confined within the crystal globe."

"I am very glad to have rescued the lady," he replied; "but, mother, I could not have accomplished it without your aid. Even now I am at a loss how to proceed."

The old dame looked at him, and began to chuckle.

"Marry! art not thou the Knight of the Ram's Horn? Ha! ha! hi! hi!"

So tickled did she appear at this somewhat ambiguous question that she laughed till the building trembled to its foundation, and she no sooner recovered from one guffaw than she went off into another, until it ended in a severe fit of coughing.

Samson the Nugget was rather surprised at the old lady's merriment. There really seemed nothing to laugh at. How was he to find the way to that subterraneous passage by which he had come? And, moreover, supposing he found it, how was he to convey the Princess up the steep sides of the black chasm?

The whole thing had been feasible enough if the ram's horn had still remained in his possession, but the relic had mysteriously gone from him the moment he re-entered the old woman's hut.

After many futile attempts at choking, Mother Dot recovered sufficiently to say,—

"Sir Knight, be not troubled concerning the maiden. I will find means to send ye both to Golden Cloud."

"But, dame, I repeat the place is a ruin."

"Tut! To thee it seemeth so," she answered shortly. "I will undo the spell cast upon it, and thou shalt see it in all its former magnificence. The statues shall rouse them from their long sleep and give ye welcome. I have said it."

The dame hobbled to a pretty cage, and took therefrom a beautiful ring-dove which perched tamely on her finger and began to coo. Bending her mouth towards its beak she whispered a few words, and the dove flew away and was lost to sight in a moment.

"Come, Sir Knight; come, Princess. You must now set forth on your journey to Golden Cloud," continued Mother Dot. "We will all mount upon the back of the ass, who shall bear us to Moonshine, after which you will have no difficulty in reaching your destination."

The miserable donkey gave forth a loud bray of dissent at the undue weight placed upon him, but a few sound thumps, administered with the old lady's crutch, soon quieted him. The dark night had fallen round them ere they reached the frontier which divides Golden Cloud from Work-a-Day.

At this point Dame Dot dismounted, and, taking leave of the Princess and her companion, said,—

"We part here, for I cannot cross this line. Remember me to His Majesty and the Queen. Farewell!"

The crone vanished, together with the ass, and left the King's daughter and her champion standing on the threshold of two worlds—the known and unknown.

On this borderland they beheld on one side a dim, imperfect light, out of which came voices filled with groans and sobs. The air trembled with countless sighs, upborne from millions of aching hearts; but the rush and the roar, and the hurry-skurry of tumult and bustle swallowed up the sounds. The other side gleamed soft and clear, with roseate shadows. There was no cry of pain, no wail of despair there.

"This is our way," the Princess said, and they left the obscure reflection behind them and went onward into the light.

## CHAPTER V.

### GOLDEN CLOUD.

AWAY beyond the sound of tears the mortal and his companion wandered. In the distance shone the glinting crest of a winding river, and as they drew near it the King's daughter clapped her hands together in rapture. "Look, look!" she said. "This is Golden Cloud. It is my home."

"Golden Cloud! Where?" The wondering gaze of the Australian youth turned east, west, south, and north. According to the landmarks in many places, this was certainly the river over which he had chased the dwarf; but lo! how changed. Could yonder towering edifice, bristling with lofty towers and domes, be that gloomy rock where he had left his companion, Grapple, asleep?

Peaks and turrets glittered under the soft light, sending untold rays aslant terrace and fountain, and upon the bright forms of dame and cavalier promenading to and fro.

Could this far-stretching vista be that bare plain over which he had passed? This with its gleaming cascades whose ripplings rivalled the lullaby of the bulbul? This with its leafy arches, and long, winding avenues, looped with clustering vines, whose stems were bent 'neath fruited gems? What bowers of green, bedecked with diamond drops and pearls of May dew!

Down where the stream flowed, the firmament, with its clustering hosts of stars, was mirrored on the liquid floor; while o'er the intervening space there floated sounds that might have ravished the senses even of a German Jew.

Cadence of bird and insect never fell before so soft and dulcet upon heaven-tuned ears. From its hundred windows the palace of King Golden Cloud beamed forth with light and beauty to welcome back its lost daughter. Welcome from bud and blossom, ringed with fire-flies, and whose ever-changing shimmer flashes a rainbow-hued light to guide their steps.

Glorious Golden Cloud! Many of us poor, fading weeds of sorrow would fain climb thy hill-top, if but to rest our weary souls for one brief moment in thy quiet groves. Oh! what sordid slaves are we who worship at those iron gates, whose recompense are wrinkled brows and silvered hair. Great Fetish of the world, the flesh, and the devil, I bow the knee to thee no more. Day by day I hear the cry of groaning thousands, that struggle for a bare existence around thy temple, calling to thee in vain. In vain they call, and vain thy power to help them. Oh thou cold and doubly-cursed humbug of the teeming world.

Standing there amidst the circle of things pure and beautiful, the Knight of the Ram's Horn beheld the approach of a pretty ring-dove towards them, with a grand barge of state following across the river. The boat drew up almost at their feet, and Silverhaze cried out, "See, this is the King's Chamberlain, Sir Bumble Bee Popgun."

As the damsel spoke, an aged figure ascended from the boat, and doffing his jewelled hat, bent low before her. "The King of Golden Cloud hath mourned for his Pearl—his child," he said in mellifluous accents.

Princess Silverhaze smiled, and stooping, whispered something in his ear, then entered the barge on the arm of her doughty knight.

Over the stream they went and up the hill at the farther side, which presented overhead a leafy arcade, where myriads of glow-worms infused a coloured sheen athwart the brilliant uniforms of the King's Guards who walled the way up to the very gates of the palace. A great concourse of nobles thronged the entrance to the royal residence and cheered the Princess as she passed round on the arm of our hero. Sir Bumble Bee led the way through throngs of bowing lackeys to the King's chamber—a large hall of state—where, seated on a magnificent dais, our hero beheld the King and Queen of Golden Cloud waiting to embrace their daughter. The chamber was thronged with ladies and gentlemen. The former wore purple robes, with blue and white mantles, which floated about with the faintest breath. Many who stood in the presence of the Queen had robes like silver, and each had a brilliant star fixed in her hair. The Nugget noticed these were most beautiful women, their complexions seeming to take the brilliancy from the light by which they were surrounded. The young Knight of the Ram's Horn saw all this at a glance, for he had an eye for the beautiful, but his vision could not take in half the things that were around him.

For some considerable time he appeared to have been forgotten, so great was the excitement on the return of the Princess. But when the stir had somewhat subsided, the King's daughter briefly detailed the exploits of our hero; how he had not only rescued her from the hands of the wicked dwarf Dusk, but that he by his courage had restored the kingdom of Golden Cloud.

More than we have space to detail, Silverhaze said in our hero's favour, and he was led forward to the throne, where the Queen embraced him and seated him on her footstool. The King, not to be outdone on this occasion, made a speech in praise of courage generally, and of the courage displayed by the Nugget in particular. This oration lasted some six hours and a quarter, and occupied about twenty-seven columns in the *Shadow Land Observer*.

The return of Silverhaze and the restoration of Golden Cloud caused universal rejoicing throughout the land. His Majesty was so well pleased with Nugget that he conferred upon him the Order of the Moon and the rank of Prince, and to crown all, said he should marry Princess Silverhaze. And they were married.

Ah, me! Wonderful, amazingly wonderful, the rank and splendour of that wedding-day! But it was over at last, and the lovers were left alone to enjoy their billing and cooing together.

* * * * *

"Come, Samson, wake up, man. Are you going to sleep all Christmas Day?" cried a gruff voice. And the Nugget, sitting up and rubbing his eyes, saw that he was still in the drive of the gold mine, with his relieving mate standing over him.

The poor fellow—HAD ONLY DREAMED.

# TWILIGHT.

## CHAPTER I.

### BARON THIMBLE.

A WINTER night, with a thick fog rising above the Sandridge marshes, and spreading itself over the city of Melbourne. People released from toil were hurrying home to tea and a pleasant fireside. Others, who neither toil nor spin, and had no home or fireside, glided slowly and noiselessly through the mist like ghosts, or stood shivering before the damp window-panes or lit-up shops and dining-rooms, feasting their hungry eyes on the good things within.

Business in the city was very dull, and money very scarce. Money is scarce at all times with a great many mortals, I am aware, but the present depression was felt everywhere throughout the colony.

Tom Brock, the barber, standing in his little

shop at the corner of Gertrude Street Fitzroy, felt the hardness of the times as keenly as any member of the community, inasmuch as Tom had a large family of growing children to provide for, and customers had been anything but numerous of late. Indeed, the poor shaver was beginning to think that the primeval fashion of suffering the hair and beard to grow in wild luxuriance on the heads and faces of his race had become the order of the day, and from henceforth he could exclaim with Shakespeare's gallant Moor—"Othello's occupation's gone."

On this winter night the barber was alone in his shop, busy stropping his razors for want of more lucrative employment. Like most of his craft, Tom Brock was a great talker. It was part and parcel of his stock-in-trade ; and, by the way, it is wonderful to note upon what a variety of subjects barbers can talk. Our hero was no exception to the rule in this respect. Having no one in the place to engage in conversation, he ceased stropping, and gazing into the large mirror opposite, addressed himself to what he saw there with charming irony in his tone.

"You're a handsome fellow, Tom Brock, a very pretty fellow indeed. Only I'm afraid looks won't go for much in this case. Here you are from eight o'clock this morning, and you've almost earned one and sixpence, according to the multiplication table. Just fancy this grand sum of eighteen pence per diem, sir, for the maintenance of eleven persons —father, mother, and nine young Brocks, whose appetites this cold weather are something to astonish Soyer the Frenchman. Don't smile at me, sir; I'm in no humour for jesting. Humph! how foolish to try and quarrel with one's shadow! Yet I've known men do that, before to-night."

He settled himself down with a sigh in the easy chair, and crossed his legs one over the other. "I wonder if the portrait and the superscription of Her Majesty the Queen is still upon the coinage of this realm?" continued the barber, speaking at the image in the mirror. "It's such a time since I handled a golden coin that, upon my life, I almost forget what they are like; perhaps that is the reason why I feel such an uncontrollable desire to look upon one at this moment. Nay, not one, but several—in short, several hundreds. Pooh, what rubbish you're talking, Tom Brock, you penniless rascal!"

The poor barber smiled at the idea of the thing, and the fellow in the mirror smiled in company. "Ready cash is a very handy thing to have at one's command, especially when it is urgently needed, as in my case," said Tom, looking sternly at his reflection. "I've often heard fellows sneer at money, and call it strange names; yet I've noted that these same revilers were always mighty eager to gather it in when they have had an opportunity. Moreover, I——"

"'SHAVE, OR HAIR CUT, SIR?' ASKED THE BARBER."

Brock the barber paused suddenly in his soliloquy; for he beheld within the radius of the looking-glass another form besides the reflection of himself. A little man, with a peculiar cast of face and features, stood behind the chair, with his arms akimbo, and his old-looking head on one side, listening greedily to the barber's utterances.

"Good-evening, sir," said Tom, starting to his feet. "Cold night?"

The little man only grinned like a monkey in reply.

"Shave, or hair cut, sir?" asked the barber, rubbing his lean hands with professional expectancy.

"Shave?" echoed the customer in a voice like a croaking raven. "Do I look as if I wanted shaving? No man shall take me by the nose, and I know you can't shave without doing *that*."

"No offence, sir. Shall I cut your hair?"

"Yes, Tom Brock. Cut it short, very short." And the wee fellow chuckled heartily as he divested himself of a cloak, in which he had been wrapped from head to heel, and seated himself in the chair before the mirror. The new-comer, although very small for his age, was quite cool and self-possessed. He gave all manner of directions respecting the mode in which he required his hair trimmed, made faces at the glass, and laughed at the grimaces reflected there.

Tom Brock had had many queer customers during the twelve years he had been in business, but he had never seen such a quaint, small mite of a man as this one before him. In fixing the wrapper about his shoulders Tom could scarcely repress an exclamation of surprise at the colour and texture of his companion's apparel. Of what material were they composed—cloth, tweed, silk, cotton? No; mortal warp or weft never manufactured such fabrics. Some other agency—subtle and mysterious as many unexplained things we see around us—had perchance woven these articles. For in this lower world there are cloaks much less substantial than a fairy's jerkin—cloaks for which Dr. Johnson and his followers have been unable to find a name, but which are indispensable to many of us in our daily lives.

Had the barber been less engaged in taking stock of the manner and appearance of his strange customer, he might have discovered at once that to shorten this fellow's hair was an utter impossibility, for as fast as the keen scissors severed the long, yellow locks the particles became instantly attached again. The barber's eyes were too intent watching the grimaces in the mirror to observe the startling fact.

"Been long in the colony, sir?" insinuated he, by way of opening a conversation.

The wee man chuckled mightily, and narrowly

escaped having a portion of his ear severed by the barber's sharp scissors.

"I know the colony, Tom Brock," he replied. "No one better. Ha, ha!"

The hairdresser was staggered, but he came again to the charge.

"Beautiful hair, yours, sir, fine and soft as silk. It doesn't seem to be much shorter, after all I've cut off."

"Cut it short, Tom. Ho, ho, ho!"

"Very dull times, sir," said Tom, not relishing his customer's disagreeable laugh.

"It's very dull indeed for *you*, Tom Brock," answered the wee man, with a knowing leer.

"Why for me, sir?"

"Because the lease of your shop expires next Monday, Tom, and you haven't a penny saved to renew it. That's why," responded the customer quietly.

Some people when they are astonished can be tumbled over with a feather, but it would have taken a blow from a large stick to have knocked our hero down. He appeared rooted to the boards, and his eyes and mouth opened considerably.

"Very good, sir. You're a wizard. Perhaps you have no objection to tell me what I had for dinner to-day!" ejaculated Tom, when he found the use of his tongue.

"Not in the least. You hadn't anything, my friend. Your mind was not upon eating to-day, but rather the consideration of where boots for the children are to come from—a bonnet for Mrs. B. likewise, the cash for your business, eh? Care has taken away your appetite, Tom. Ha, ha! I know. No one knows better than Thimble. That's me."

The comb and scissors fell from the barber's hand to the floor.

"Want to know anything else, Tom Brock?" asked the visitor.

"Nothing more, thank ye," replied the barber in a bewildered tone.

"Listen to me, then." And the little fellow faced about in the chair. "I am Baron Thimble, of Faydell Twilight. Ours is a vast kingdom in the centre of Australia, of which very little is known by man. The Anglo-Saxon has penetrated into every corner of the known globe, and thrust his inquisitive nose into the socket of the North Pole, but he has never set foot in the land of Twilight. Now I need your services, Tom Brock, and if you will promise to go with me, I will reward you handsomely."

"Twilight," repeated Brock thoughtfully. "I never heard mention of such a country before."

"I trow not," replied Baron Thimble, smiling. "Nevertheless, it is a great realm, whose people have often visited these cities, reared on the sea border. Thou art poor, and in need, and faith, I repeat, I have need of thee."

"How long will you require me?"

"For just one moon. No more."

"And the reward?" inquired Tom eagerly.

"Two hundred golden coins."

"Thank you, I am at your service. Stop! Is Twilight far away, Baron Thimble?"

"Yes, but our conveyance will be swift and safe. Thou wilt go?"

"With the greatest pleasure, sir."

"Enough! Here are one hundred sovereigns in part payment of my promise." And the Twilight nobleman drew forth a heavy purse and counted the money into the barber's palm. "Go home at once and bank the money with thy wife; then meet me afterwards on the right bank of the river Yarra, beyond the Lunatic Asylum. You understand?"

And the Baron, chuckling to himself, folded his poncho about his person, and strode out at the doorway.

Tom Brock could hardly believe but that the whole affair had been a joke. There lay the money, though. That was real enough. And he felt it was no joke to have it in his possession. So he packed up his shaving appliances in a bag, closed his shop, and went home to his better half.

## CHAPTER II.

### PRINCE PICNIC.

THE inhabitants of Twilight have a more facile means of transition than the sons of men. While we have our steamboats, railways, telegraphs, and all other nurslings of science as our slaves, the races of the dim region can command the services of the powerful Air King *Fancy*. Swifter is he than the Wind, and stronger than the fabled Griffin of the Ancients. He can accommodate any number and all manner of travellers at a moment's notice.

Baron Thimble, standing by the Yarra bank, invoked the rapid harbinger to his aid, and when Tom Brock the barber joined him there, they were fully prepared to start on their voyage.

"*Humbug-loo-boo! Tictoleroo! Pish-bosh! Fudge!*"

cried the son of Twilight, and they were off. The electrical current, girdling the storm-tossed waters, where ships are broken and engulfed, could not outpace the conveyance of the fairy and the barber. The most elegant saloon could not afford more comfort than those trance-stuffed cushions upon which they reclined and gazed out upon the newly brightened landscape.

Then the fairy man spoke and unfolded his mission.

"I am the Baron Thimble. Know, O mortal, that the wise Prince Picnic is Ruler and Governor of Twilight. The Prince hath a beautiful daughter named Bi-ba-be-bi, which in the language of the country implies the Lady Lollypop. Twelve months ago, while the Prince was hunting in the Leap Frog Mountains, he was made prisoner by a huge, powerful chief of the Baboon country, named Gorilla, who demanded the Prince's daughter in marriage, as ransom. My master consented to the terms, but begged that Gorilla would not press his suit for the space of one year and a day, so that Bi-ba-be-bi might be prepared for the ceremony. The monster agreed. And now, the time specified having elapsed, the horrid creature has crossed the mountains to demand his bride."

The voice of Baron Thimble trembled with

emotion as he continued: "Prince Picnic is full of sorrow, for he cannot think of suffering his lovely daughter to mate with such a monster as Gorilla. Bribes have been offered, gold and silver and gems, besides a large tract of territory known as Shadowsflit, bordering on our country, but the monster will have nothing in lieu of the lady."

"Why don't you call out the volunteers, and drive the beast back into the mountains?" inquired the barber.

"Ah, there lies the difficulty," answered Thimble. "The Governor of Twilight has never broken his word to man or monster, and he will not go from it in this instance. The nobles and churchmen have tried to persuade him that, under the circumstances, he is not bound to redeem his word with Gorilla; but he will not listen to our advice, and I'm afraid the lovely girl, Lady Lollypop, will be sacrificed."

"What is the Baboon chief like?" asked the barber.

"Tall as a giant, and as strong as a dozen giants combined," replied his companion. "The Prince quartered him in the summer palace, and the rogue has almost torn it down piecemeal. He has eaten up the shrubs and flowers, and destroyed every animal within his reach."

"Has Lady Lollypop seen her affianced husband?"

"No; poor Bi-ba-be-bi remains as yet in blissful ignorance of the fact, yet to-morrow the whole matter must be made known to her, except——" and the Baron paused, and looked fixedly at Tom Brock.

"Except what?" said the barber.

"Except you aid us," rejoined the fairy. "We held a Council yesterday—Gaboon, the Prince's jester, being President. The Chairman, who understands the manners, customs, and language of Gorilla-land, stated that this monster was not in his opinion a real native Gorilla, inasmuch as the beings of the Baboon regions had only four toes, whereas the visitor had five; further, in conversing with the intended husband of the fair Bi-ba-be-bi, he had discovered that the creature spoke the language of the country with a strong foreign accent—these, together with other matters he did not wish at that meeting to particularise, induced him (the Chairman) to conclude that the monster was other than what he appeared, and that the only way to test the truth or otherwise of his suggestion, with reference to the unwelcome guest, would be to engage a smart barber to shave the Gorilla from head to heel. I need scarcely add that the proposition of the President was unanimously agreed to. And here you are!"

Wee Baron Thimble chuckled and rubbed his hands together until the joints cracked again.

"Why, you surely didn't engage me to shave a Gorilla?" cried the poor barber in astonishment.

"I certainly did, Tom Brock."

"What! All over—body and all?" inquired he, with starting eyeballs.

"Body, head and feet, Tom. Wherever there is a hair you must cut it off," replied Thimble.

"Well, I've often heard of a pig being shaved, but never a Gorilla. What do you want to shave the beast for, eh?"

The Baron remained thoughtful for a moment ere he replied. "It will be a sure test to prove whether this monster is really the chief of the Baboon realm or not," he said. "If he is not, so much the better for Lollypop, and if he is the real Simon Pure, his enormous strength will depart with his heavy coat. He will become docile, and we can then dress him as becomes the bridegroom of a Princess. That is the opinion of Gaboon."

"Bother Gaboon!" cried the barber. "I only wish the President of the Council had to shave the creature, that's all."

"There are no barbers in Twilight," answered

Thimble; "else I had not come to thee; besides, thou hast received thy reward."

"This monster may kill me," replied Tom.

"True. Then again he may not. Come, man, whatever thou may'st value thyself at shall be paid to thee when thy task is ended. Great results hang upon thy skill and on the keen edge of thy tools. Although shaving is unknown *here*, there is a potent influence about it amongst thy race, whether it may be upon their faces or upon their consciences. Here we are at the mansion of Prince Picnic."

A charming edifice rises to view, nestling its gables and turrets 'midst clouds of richest foliage, upon whose glistening tops rest every shade of green, with brown and russet and yet a colour of amber between, encircling the wave like hills in the distance. Kingdom of Twilight! how I love thee! Not as a stranger do I enter thy gates. I have been here before, long, long ago, when the years were young and full of promise for me; when she was by my side who was too frail, too good for earth. Here we have lingered silently, side by side, while the nightingale warbled forth its soft notes in love for the rose, and the roses gave forth their fragrance until the air became an essence of perfume. Oh, sweet bird of Twilight, thy song yet fills the air, but silent and cold the fond heart that beat in unison with thy sweet music. Will she listen for thy singing when the twilight gathers its shadows o'er her lowly grave on the hillside? Oh, nightingale! oh, twilight memories! Ye preach to my yearning soul more eloquently than words of man. Patience, love, hope, are borne to me upon your voice, and fall gently as the breath of mercy and forgiveness upon the quickened sense, that sees revealed for one brief moment a glimpse of Paradise and its forms of unperishable glory.

The approach of the two travellers was observed by the captain of the guard at the palace gates, who immediately sent a message to the Prince; whereupon, as soon as they arrived they were ushered into the presence of the Ruler of Twilight, who received the Baron and the barber very graciously. Refreshments were ordered to be set before them, and when Tom had satisfied the cravings of hunger, Prince Picnic asked him many questions respecting his journey, and desired to inspect the articles in the bag. While Prince Picnic was engaged with the razors and lather box, our hero had time to have a good look at him. He appeared much smaller than the Baron, and a trifle older looking, yet the Prince was still what many ladies would term a handsome fellow. His white pointed beard was very long and strongly scented, yet his eyes were as keen as a hawk, and his step as supple and light as a boy of fifteen. If Tom Brock had wondered at the richness and texture of Baron Thimble's clothing, he wondered still more at the magnificence of Prince Picnic's dressing-gown, and also at the lavish display of pure gold in everything he saw about the room. In fact, the barber had yet to learn that the country was one vast gold mine, which in the absence of other metals was employed for everything in common use.

It was time to retire to rest when the Prince broke up the audience.

The Baron conducted Tom to an elegant sleeping apartment. "The Gorilla has found his way here," he said at parting. "The beast has selected the sward of the lawn in preference to a bed. Remember, your task must be finished before the assembling of the Court to-morrow. Sleep well. Good-night."

## CHAPTER III.

### LADY LOLLYPOP.

The barber was honoured with a perfumed bath ere he retired to rest, which caused him to sleep soundly until daylight began to peep through the windows of his chamber. His slumbers would have been prolonged had it not been for a feeling of sudden pain across the bridge of his nose. He awoke hastily, and beheld the form of a very ancient dame standing by his bedside. That puppet, known as the spouse of Mr. Punch, was the only creature that our hero could liken her to, as she bent her thin profile over him and held up her skinny hand in token of silence and attention. Fixing her keen eyes upon Tom, she chanted, rather than spoke, the following incantation :—

> "Draw a circle round the beast
> When he sleeps in peaceful rest;
> If strong thy arm and keen thy blade
> So thy task is easy made.
> Shave the monster, head and toe,
> Round him fold this robe of snow;
> Then lead him forth towards the Throne.
> Fe-fi-fum, my charm is done."

Ere the last words were well out of her mouth

the old dame vanished like a puff of smoke—when or how Tom Brock had no idea whatever. He rubbed his eyes, and was under the impression that the whole thing was an illusion, until his glance rested upon a square white wrapper lying at the foot of the bed. He sprang up immediately, and found a soft cloak large enough to robe a giant. There was no fancy about *that*, at any rate. He dressed himself hastily, at the same time attempting to repeat the utterances of his strange visitor:—

> "'Draw a circle round the beast
> When he sleeps in peaceful rest.'

Very good," he muttered quickly; "there may be a charm in these words that I cannot conceive. I have a very dangerous task before me, and I'll try it. Luckily this is just the time of day to catch Mr. Gorilla asleep. What's the next line?—

> "'If strong thy arm and keen thy blade
> So thy task is easy made.'

Humph! I can answer for the razors. They're sharp enough to cut the throat of my ugly customer, if he tries any of his tricks: Then:—

> "'Shave the monster, head and toe,
> Round him fold this robe of snow.'

All right so far. After which I'm to lead him into the reception-hall before Prince Picnic. Just so. Now to set about it."

The barber prepared his razors and lather, and taking the white robe on his arm he went out along the broad corridor towards the garden. Within a small grass plot encircled by tall trees Tom discovered the Gorilla fast asleep. With noiseless footsteps our hero formed a wide ring round the sleeping monster with his fingers, and then stepped within the charmed circle and approached his subject. Strange to relate, the Gorilla never stirred—not even when Tom, with the taste of a genuine artist, began operations upon his capacious chin. Nature seemed hushed while the barber performed his business. Above, below, and around a deep stillness reigned, save for the scraping, grating sound of Tom Brock's blade.

Meanwhile Prince Picnic held a grand council of state in the magnificent reception-hall of his palace. Previously an edict had gone forth which summoned the rank, beauty, and fashion of the land to witness the marriage of Lady Lollypop and Gorilla. And here they were assembled for the imposing event, which should unite the Beauty and the Beast.

Ah, me! Who shall attempt to describe the splendour of that gathering? The Ruler of Twilight was seated on a throne of pure gold, which had been oxidized to every shade of colour, and wrought in the most beautiful mosaic imaginable. At her father's side reclined the Bi-ba-be-bi, receiving the homage of the young nobles and the long-bearded functionaries of state. The walls and ceiling of the throne chamber were entirely covered with wide sheets of burnished gold to reflect as mirrors. On each side of the dais there extended rank upon rank of high-born dames and courtiers robed in stuffs of silk and gold, embroidered with flowers so as to present the most perfect imitations of nature.

Soothingly soft, sweetly, lovingly soft, were the dulcet tones of the choir of fairy musicians, hidden from view—now ebbing, now flowing in tender gushes of melody. Down the sides of the lofty pillared hall a bright band of dancing fays, each as lovely as a child's dream, advanced and retired, crossed and interlaced in a whirling maze of shifting light, which defeated the eye in following their quick and graceful evolutions. Amongst that fair galaxy of beauty, Bi-ba-be-bi stood out peerless in her loveliness. Round the soft cushions on which she reclined were gathered her four handmaids, See-Saw, Hide and Seek, Marjory Daw, and Down-Dilly.

Behind the throne stood Ride-a-cock-horse, the prime minister, Gaboon, the jester, and the high officials of the kingdom. At a sign from Baron Thimble the music ceased and the dancers dispersed. Then Prince Picnic rose, and said briefly,—

"People of Twilight, I have called you together to witness the marriage of our daughter, the Lady Lollypop. I am aware that this Court had decided that our dear and lamented nephew Prince Pippin should have been her husband; but the gallant youth perished three years ago on those self-same Leap Frog Mountains where I and my retinue were captured by Gorilla. The chief of Gorilla-land is now here to claim the bond I gave him for our release."

A deep hush had fallen o'er the vast crowd as the Prince paused.

"Prince Pippin was a handsome youth and a gallant gentleman," whispered See-Saw.

"True, and our lady loved him well," replied Down-Dilly.

The daughter of Prince Picnic heard the whispering, and sighed audibly.

"Ay, but the young Prince is dead. Hush!"

"Dames and nobles," continued His Highness mournfully, "we have given our sacred word that this monster shall marry Bi-ba-be-bi. Therefore we cannot depart from that pledge in the smallest particular. What, ho there! Let the bridegroom come forth and claim his bride."

As the Ruler of Twilight uttered the words, every eye was directed towards the great folding doors at the farther end of the audience chamber, which were instantly drawn apart, and Tom Brock entered, leading the tall figure of his patient, muffled from head to feet in the white cloak.

Poor Lady Lollypop uttered a stifled shriek of fear as her gaze fell upon the muffled form of her intended lord and master.

The barber advanced with his companion to the foot of the throne, and there halted for a moment, then retired behind the throng of courtiers, leaving the closely covered monster standing alone.

"Art thou still resolved to have the Pearl of Twilight for thy wife?" asked Ride-a-cock-horse in a loud voice.

The mantled figure trembled visibly, but held his peace.

"Let the chief of Gorilla-land show himself, if he is not afraid," cried Gaboon, advancing from out of the ring of nobles by which he was surrounded. Swifter than the electrical fire athwart a thunder-cloud the folding mantle vanished from that form, and revealed—not the hateful beast, but a tall, handsome young man, robed in a superb hunting costume of the country. The gaze of Bi-ba-be-bi

"A TALL, HANDSOME YOUNG MAN, ROBED IN A SUPERB HUNTING COSTUME."

had no sooner rested upon him than she sprang from the midst of her ladies with a glad cry of recognition, and cast herself upon his bosom. "Prince Pippin! Cousin! My own dear love, you are not dead!"

Dead, not at all. Twilight is a region of

enchantment, dear readers. Dame Trot, the witch of the Leap Frog Ranges, had fallen across the young Prince while hunting in the mountains, and had changed him into a Gorilla. Such he had remained and had taken his uncle prisoner. When the news, however, of the marriage between Lady Lollypop and the supposed monster reached the old magician she relented of her wickedness by appearing at the bedside of the barber and speaking the words which annulled the charm.

There was great rejoicing at the court of Prince Picnic over the event; but the gladness and the display were increased a hundredfold when the cousins were married.

Tom Brock, loaded with substantial presents, returned home to his wife and family, and brought a piece of the wedding-cake for the former, which quite dissipated any lurking jealousy there might have been in her mind respecting his absence.

The little corner shop knows our friend the barber no more. His residence is now in the aristocratic suburb of Toorak—a magnificent mansion known as "Faydell," and for which he may thank Bi-ba-be-bi and her royal husband Prince Pippin.

# TIM.

THE sinking sun cast a soft amber-tinted radiance over the little township of Wentworth, New South Wales, as a little boy, weary and footsore with travel, knocked at a farmer's door about two miles beyond the settlement.

A kind, motherly woman who answered the knock stared with astonishment at the juvenile tramp, who blurted out in a faint voice, "If you please, ma'am, will you give me a drink of water? I'm so hungry, I really don't know where I shall sleep to-night."

The good lady laughed heartily at the little fellow's quaint request. She took him into the house, and led him into a back room, where a great fat man was seated at tea.

"Who is this, wife?" said he in a surly tone, looking at our hero.

"Only a poor boy begging some food, Mark; that's all," answered his wife meekly.

"I didn't beg, ma'am, please," said the boy quickly.

"Oh, you didn't beg?" rejoined the farmer in the same gruff voice. "Git down on that stool now."

"I came a very long way, sir, and I——" began the boy.

"Silence! Wife, take his bundle; pull off his old shoes; let him be washed; then give him his tea." The voice lost nothing of its coarse disagreeable ring as it gave the curt order, but the man's eyes looked kindly at the little wanderer " What is your name?" still gruffly.

"Tim, sir, please."

"Tim *what*? Hav'n't you another name?"

"No, sir. Nuggety Joe never called me anything else than Tim."

"And who is Nuggety Joe?" asked the farmer.

The boy played nervously with the edge of his tattered jacket for a moment, and then replied in a voice broken and unsteady with emotion, "Please, sir, father and Joe were mates on the diggings at Forbes. When the great dam broke and flooded the creek, and drowned father, mother, and little sister Jessie, Joe took care of me, and was a father to me—he was—until

he took the fever, and died, and then I——"
The child's quavering voice gave way to a fit of bitter wailing.

"Stop that!" cried the farmer, putting his handkerchief to his nose, and making that organ sound like a French horn—" stop it at once. I'll have no snivelling here."

But poor Tim sobbed on; and notwithstanding all the womanly sympathy of the farmer's wife, she could not stay the torrent. Not yet in his "teens," the brave lad walked over two hundred miles, suffering hunger and pain with the courage of a Spartan; but he had no courage to put back the tears that swelled upwards at the remembrance of that rude, unlettered, dead digger, who had loved him, and had taken him to his bosom for Christ's sake, and who had now gone to receive his reward.

All things have an end, so the fountain of Tim's eyes became dry again ere the tea was over. Before the lad was sent to bed, the farmer said, "Look here, boy, I think I can give you something to do on my farm. Mind, I'll set you a task the first thing in the morning; if you perform it to my satisfaction, and you likewise prove yourself an honest, trustworthy youngster, why, you shall never want a home or a friend while Mark Wilson lives. Now, wife, put him to bed."

The good dame led Tim to a small attic bedroom, which contained, amongst other things, a beautiful parrot in a stout wire cage.

"Cockie" had evidently been enjoying a nap, for he shook himself at sight of the intruders, and sent forth from his bill a volley of strange sounds, in true imitation of a person just aroused from slumber. Mrs. Wilson kissed our hero and retired, but she had hardly closed the door before the bird began to flap his wings and crow like a rooster.

"A funny parrot," muttered Tim. "I wonder if it can talk?"

"Of course it can," answered Cockie, eyeing him through the bars of the cage. The lad rubbed his eyes, and stared at the bird in the cage for fully three minutes without speaking a word, so great was his consternation. "Don't stare, Tim; it's very rude to stare," continued the bird gravely. "People in this colony have a bad habit of staring you out of countenance, I am sorry to say."

"Why, you can talk like a man," cried the boy in his astonishment.

"Certainly; much better than some men, I

trust. Pray come here and scratch me, Tim," cried the parrot coaxingly.

Little Tim obeyed very cautiously, and in fear and trembling.

"That is delightful," said Cockie.

"It's wonderful," muttered poor Tim.

"What is wonderful, sir? Can't parrots talk?"

"Some of them can, but not like you."

Oh! but I'm not a parrot, I'm a fairy."

"A fairy?" cried the boy, agape with wonder. "Are you really?"

"Truly I am. One of the Lake George fairies. Xanthine, our Queen, turned me into a parrot, five years ago, through her foolish jealousy, and here I've been caged up ever since with this great beak upon my face, which quite disfigures me."

"What a shame! Can't you get back again to your friend at Lake George?" cried the boy.

"Yes, for Queen Xanthine is dead, and I can now return in safety, if you will help me," replied the bird.

"Me! how can I help you?" answered little Tim.

"I will tell you," rejoined the elfin. "You must know, boy, that every one of us could help each other if we would. The rich can help the poor, and the poor the wealthy; yea, even the smallest can render assistance to the strong and powerful, as was the case with the lion and the mouse. Now, I can prove how I can render you a service. Judge. Didn't the master say he would set you a task in the morning?"

"He did," replied Tim in wonder.

"Very well. The task is to milk a bad-tempered, touchy old cow called 'Peggy.' The beast, who is a splendid milker, is the torment and plague of the farmer's life. She has kicked him until he is afraid to approach her, and every one, man, woman, and boy, who attempts to milk Peggy is sure to be upset. It has proved useless to tie her by the leg and the tail—the wicked rogue would find a way of defeating her enemies before the milking was ended."

"Are you sure that I shall have to try to milk Peggy in the morning?" inquired Tim.

"Quite certain," replied the elfin.

"Then I—I think I had better go away now, at once, before the morning, don't you?" said the lad ruefully.

"No, I don't, because I can tell you how to overcome the antics of this refractory cow."

"How?"

"I will tell you upon one condition," replied the fairy parrot, rubbing its beak reflectively.

"What condition?" asked Tim.

"That you set me free as soon as you have completed your task to-morrow."

"It's a bargain," replied little Tim readily. "I can easily get the farmer another parrot—a real bird, you know—and then there will be no harm done."

"Very good. Now listen. On the gable of this house there grows a creeper with a pale blue flower. In the morning, when they call you, go and gather a small wreath of this plant, and when the wicked cow is bailed up ready for milking, place the vine around her horns, and you may take the word of an Australian fairy that Peggy will stand as quiet as a mouse until you have drained her teats as dry as a corn cob."

"Lor! how simple!" replied Tim.

"All knowledge is simple, boy, when you once acquire it. You'll not forget my instructions?"

"No, I thank you. I shall remember."

"Kiss Cockie, then, say your prayers like a good boy, and go to bed. Good-night."

Tim wished to ask the fairy bird a hundred questions, but after it had said good-night it would not utter another word, so the boy went to bed and fell asleep.

The sun was up before him in the morning.

Yet Tim managed to get down into the garden and cut a slender tendril from the creeper, which he formed into a small hoop, just as the farmer's voice was heard calling him.

Twenty cows had to be milked every morning at the farm, and Tim heard a great deal of shouting and bellowing, and clanking of milk-cans, which proceeded from a yard at hand, enclosed with a high fence and into which the cattle had been driven.

The farmer led our hero into the enclosure, and pointing to where the ill-tempered short-horn stood, with her head in the bail, said briefly, "Sit down and milk that cow."

The boy went up to Peggy, who gave a loud bellow at sight of him. He placed the vine around her horns, then sat down to his task. Mark Wilson stood ready to pick the boy up in case the cow knocked him over; but the beast never moved until the boy had drawn every drop of milk from her teats. The good farmer was filled with amazement, and cried out, "Twenty-five boys and ten men have all tried to milk Peggy, and not one of them has succeeded but you. Therefore, from this moment, I will adopt you as my son, Tim, and you shall marry my little girl Amy, by-and-by, and I will leave you the farm as a wedding present." And the farmer kept his word.

When Tim went upstairs to set the parrot free, he found the bird transformed into a beautiful wee lady, whom he politely lifted out of the cage. She thanked him, and made him a graceful curtsey as she vanished out of the window.

# THREE SPARROWS.

TOBY GRUMBLETON worked with his uncle down in one of the deepest mines in Ballarat. If you had searched the whole district in that gold hunting region, you couldn't have found a more selfish, lazy, and disobedient boy than Toby. In consequence of his surly and complaining disposition his companions had bestowed upon him the nickname of "Toby the Growler," and he well deserved the title; for a greater snivelling, discontented youth never existed.

One day, while at work in the mine, Toby was ordered to gather together all the blunt tools and send them up to the surface to be sharpened. As usual, Toby began to grumble, whereupon his uncle gave him a good thrashing, and the "Growler" ran off into one of the usual drives or passages of the mine to indulge in a sulking fit. Of the many dark and wide caverns underground, none in the whole pit was so large and so gloomy and dismal as the one in which "Toby the Growler" had taken refuge, yet the boy had not been there long before he became aware of a strange yellow-coloured glow lighting up the drive. Looking up, he beheld a little old dwarf, with a lamp in his hand, standing over him. Such a

"'GET UP, TOBY THE GROWLER, AND FOLLOW ME.'"

plain, ugly-looking creature Toby had never seen before, though there are any number of queer-looking fellows at Ballarat. The intruder was small, not nearly so tall as Toby, but his head was a rasper, and appeared as if it had belonged to several ancient individuals in succession, the eyes very red, and omitting a fiery glow. He was attired in a suit of brown russet, with a long sugar-loaf hat, and a crutch staff.

"Get up, Toby the Growler, and follow me," cried the dwarf in a brief tone, and looking at him with those horrid eyes. Toby felt inclined to disobey, but his heart sank within him at sight of the creature, and he therefore followed, grumbling as he went, and wondering where the ugly little humpback would lead him. Of one thing the boy was certain—that the end of the subterranean passage would effectually bar the progress of the unwelcome visitor; but the dim cave seemed to extend and open out before them as they proceeded, until it took the shape of a long railway tunnel, from which they at length emerged into the bright open sunlight, beaming down upon a landscape fairer than a child's dream. The sudden transit from what appeared to be the bowels of a great high mountain to the noonday light almost blinded our friend Toby; but the dwarf touched him with his staff, and lo! the boy beheld a charming country teeming with life and beauty. Here were soft grassy spots, shaded by trees bending with ripe and golden-hued fruit; yonder a range of hills clothed with richest verdure, and at the feet of which a broad lake gleamed like a burnished shield. There were swans on the lake, and birds of bright plumage on the trees and in the air, and birds everywhere around.

"What place is this, sir?" cried Toby in amazement.

"This is the land of the three sparrows," answered the dwarf with a smile. "Look there; that little white building is the home of '*Test*,' the eldest of the three; yonder by the water is the palace of '*Try*,' while on the hills over there you can see the castle of '*Cure*,' the youngest."

"Are they real sparrows, sir?" asked Toby.

"No, boy, only in form. They are Australian elves. Every twenty years the great body of elfins in this country transform three of their number into the shape of sparrows, to govern this land, and also for other purposes, of which you may judge for yourself." Saying which, the dwarf caught the Growler in his arms, and in an instant they were standing by the white palace on the lake. All the windows and doors were wide open, so the dwarf entered with his companion and conducted him to a large room where Test sat perched on the back of an armchair. He seemed a well-feathered, plump old bird and wore spectacles.

"Ah, Grip, my trusty messenger," he cried, "I see you have returned with the Growler; take him hence and test him in the usual way."

"Very well, your Excellency," and the dwarf bent low in obeisance and retired. He led Toby away into a large empty hall, and standing him up beside the door, said, "Toby, Toby, shut your eyes and see what Fate will send you." The Growler closed his eyes, when the voice of the dwarf was again heard. "Toby, Toby, open your eyes and see what Fate *has* sent you."

The boy opened his eyes and beheld the most magnificent apartment it is possible to conceive. Tables with marble tops, inlaid with gold, were loaded with choice fruits and lollies, and by some enchantment the boy's ragged clothes were changed to a gorgeous suit of crimson velvet, bordered with pearls, and several servants stood at hand ready to do his bidding.

"Ah, this is as it should be!" cried the delighted Toby. "I shall never grumble again if I am to live like this. Here are guns to shoot with; dogs to hunt with; horses to ride, and plenty of fishing in the lake. Ah! I shall be thoroughly satisfied now." And the Growler set about enjoying himself.

But alas! for human resolves. The fruit made

Toby ill; one of the horses threw him and hurt his leg; he nearly shot himself with his gun; and was all but drowned in the lake while fishing; and so he began to complain worse than before. But the moment he did so, the splendid scene vanished from before him in the twinkling of an eye, and he discovered himself in the bare and empty room again, with only his dirty rags, and the dwarf standing grinning beside him.

"Come along with me, Toby the Growler," cried the old fellow in a mocking tone; and before the boy could refuse he was borne away to the palace of Try. This old and venerable sparrow was deep in the pages of the *Observer* when Grip entered with Toby.

"Whom have we here?" he inquired, addressing the dwarf.

"Please, your Worship, this is a mortal who has been tested by your Worship's brother, and has failed," answered Grip.

"What is his special defect?"

"Grumbling, your Worship."

"Humph! a common quality among mortals, more especially with farmers and boys. Try him without delay."

With the quickness of a shifting scene in a

magic-lantern Toby was transferred to a cottage in a lonely valley, occupied by an old lady and gentleman, who welcomed him as if he had been their own son, and procured for him all that he could desire. The whole day was one round of pleasure and enjoyment, and the boy expressed himself grateful and satisfied with his position. One simple act he had to perform in return for all this kindness, and that was to draw seven buckets of water from a well every morning, for the use of the cottage. Yet Toby the Growler, unmindful of past experience, began to grumble again, and once more he found himself by the lake with the dwarf at his elbow.

"For the last time, come with me, Toby the Growler," he cried in a terrible voice, while his red flaming eyes shot out flashes like fire. The boy felt utterly powerless to resist, and swift as a streak of lightning he was carried to the gloomy abode of Cure, the youngest of the three sparrows. The castle was as dark as a dungeon, but the guide found his way within to the reception-hall, where Cure, in regal feathers, sat surrounded by a guard of crows bearing torches.

"Who is this?" inquired the youngest sparrow sternly.

"A grumbling boy, your Highness,"

"Let him be cured. Take him away."

The words were scarcely spoken ere poor Toby found himself instantly transformed into a donkey with long ears. He was on a hard, hilly road, dragging a heavy dray after him loaded with firewood. At first the lad felt somewhat doubtful respecting the sudden transformation, but a smart thump across his buttock soon convinced him he was no longer an idle boy, but a beast of burden, with a cruel youth for his master, who beat and bruised him unmercifully with a thick stick. Oh! the long and weary hours he had to toil, while the miserable food he had to eat made him weep, and wet the winkers with his tears. He thought of his uncle and his home, and all the many kindnesses he had received, and had repaid with complaints and grumblings, and he vowed earnestly, and with true penitence, that if ever he got back again to the mine and to his kind relative, he would avoid complaining for the rest of his life.

With this firm resolve came another sudden shifting in the magic scene. So sudden was it that Toby rubbed his eyes, and found himself in that self-same narrow drive in the mine at Ballarat, with his uncle shaking him by the collar, and telling him that it was time to go to the surface.

Toby is a man now, and is married and has several children; and if one of these begins to grumble, he does not forget to remind them of the Three Sparrows.

# KING DUNCE.

ONLY a careless, stupid boy perched on a high stool within the schoolroom, trying to learn his lesson, long after his companions had been dismissed to their several homes. Only the biggest dunce at Slate-em's Academy, who wouldn't try, like other boys, to master his tasks —not because he hadn't the ability to do so, but because he wanted to be a King. Yes, dear readers, Noel Biffin, son of Jack Biffin, the tinsmith, wanted to be a King. Nothing less would satisfy him. No, not even the rank of Duke or Prince; so, instead of minding his lessons, young Biffin drew Kings on his slate and in his copybook, and was therefore compelled to ride the wooden horse after school hours.

It was a very beautiful evening, with a grand sunset glow flooding Slate-em's Academy, and wrapping the Dunce round and round as with an amber-coloured mantle, orange tinted. The old usher, nodding in his chair, was quite unconscious of the halo which played round and about his bald, venerable head, and made him appear for one brief moment like one of the Apostles. The good, patient old man was tired with the heat, and weary with the incessant chatter of the boys, and so he dozed in comfort, and saw not the wee, shapely creature who entered at the window and approached the boy as he stood upon the stool and bent the knee before him. Although small, the stranger was very handsome, and decked from head to heel in bright, glittering armour, with a crimson plume adorning his helmet.

"May it please your gracious Majesty," he said, doffing his helmet, "my name is Popgun—Sir Guy Fawkes Popgun, Knight—one of your Majesty's subjects from the realm of Shadowland." The Dunce nearly fell from the stool in amazement at the strange words. He looked towards the still sleeping master, and from him to the armour-clad Knight at his feet, and replied in a low tone, "Hush! Don't speak so loud. I haven't learnt my lesson yet; if he wakens he'll thrash me. Now, what do you want?"

"Pardon, your liege," rejoined the Knight respectfully, "I am sent as ambassador from the good people of Shadowland to inform your

"Speeding away across the country as swift as the wind."

Majesty that you have been unanimously elected monarch of our wide and spacious dominions, and I beg that it may please you to allow me to conduct you thither without delay."

"A King! Am I really a King after all?" cried Biffin, jumping from the stool.

"Every inch a King, your Majesty," replied Sir Guy Fawkes Popgun, replacing his headpiece. "Will your liege follow me?"

"Stop, where is Shadowland?" inquired the boy.

"On the borders of Fancy, where dwell my kindred, the Australian elves. Fairyland will have none but a mortal to reign over her. Come, your Majesty." And with a dignified bearing the Elfin Knight strode past the slumbering usher, and led the newly-elected Majesty of Elfland out at the door, which opened at their approach. Beyond the school, out on the open play-ground, stood two fine-looking emus, splendidly caparisoned, and ready for a journey; and before young Biffin knew what he was about he and his companion were mounted thereon, and were speeding away across the country as swift as the wind. Small townships, hills and valleys, tracts of gloomy forests, and broad lakes appeared before them, and disappeared behind them again, before the boy could say "Jack Robinson"

Indeed, poor Biffin hadn't breath to say anything, they proceeded so swiftly. At length they came to a large sandy desert on the confines of which rose a chain of lofty mountains. After crossing the desert these mountains looked so steep and high that further progress appeared at an end, but the Knight went to a cave close by and brought forth a pair of flying horses, which flew upward with them in a moment and landed them far away on the other side in safety—and this was Shadowland of the Elfins. What poet's brain, teeming with strange wild fancies, could give expression to such a scene of loveliness as Noel the Dunce saw here? What travel-stained worshipper of Nature, traversing the girdle of the globe, ever feasted his eyes on a more glorious prospect? Not at Rome, filled as it is with monuments of man; nor at Athens, where Paul found the tablet inscribed, "To the Unknown God"; or on that Ionian Isle, where the inspired John wrote "The Revelation." Beautiful and sacred are all three to view, but I have feasted my soul on scenes equally grand and sublime in this new land where the Universal Spirit of "Our Father" seemed to rest, and attract the uplifted eyes and the inmost thoughts of the Soul to the Invisible Presence.

The flying steeds alighted in a ravine shut in by walls of fantastic rocks, peaked and turreted like the gable of some old feudal castle. Here a mounted escort, composed of the potent and mighty of the empire, awaited their coming, and led the King upwards to a grassy platform, shaded by a patch of hoary trees, where a throne built of wild-flowers had been erected for his reception. The site commanded a fine view of the surrounding country, and the elected monarch beheld with satisfaction thousands and thousands of his subjects assembled on the plains below to do him homage, and whose cheers and shouts rang far and wide when he ascended the throne to read the proclamation.

From time to time, for generations past, the Elfin Kings had to read their own proclamations, but when young Biffin received the paper from the hands of the Prime Minister his heart sank within him. His progress at school had been so slow that he was unable to read print fluently. How, then, was he to master the contents of the closely-written parchment in his hand? At that moment he would have given all his toys at home, even to his crop-eared pony, to have been able to read writing; but he couldn't read or spell, nor make anything better than a pot-hook.

"May it please your Majesty to read the proclamation to the people?" whispered Sir Guy Fawkes Popgun in the King's ear.

"I—I cannot read," replied his Majesty, trembling with shame and vexation.

"*Cannot read!*" repeated the courtiers, looking at each other. "Surely your Majesty is jesting."

"Indeed, gentlemen, I'm afraid I'm a dunce," replied Biffin sheepishly.

"A dunce, who cannot read, and yet has the silly presumption to be a King!" shouted the fairy populace in a mocking tone. "Hurrah for King Dunce! Long live King Dunce!"

And such is the uncertainty of popular favour in Elfland, that the vast assembly, who but a moment before had exhibited such hearty tokens of good-will, began to hoot and clamour in derision. They pulled the monarch from his throne, stripped him of his robes of state, and carried him to a rocky peak, where they doffed his crown and replaced it with a wreath of straw; while their shouts—"Long live King Dunce! Hurrah for King Dunce!"—once more rent the air.

In all his troubles at home, and his canings and disappointments with his lessons at school, our hero never felt so humbled and crestfallen in his life before. He would have given anything to be enabled to read and write well. And this wish would have been easily gratified, had he but paid a little attention to his books while at the Academy; but he hadn't done so, and the result was his downfall from the proud position he had so long coveted.

What availed his regrets *now*, when he was led away a prisoner, and placed in a dark cave, guarded by seven monsters, whose bodies were covered with long feathers, and who had heads like monkeys? It availed nothing that they set him hard lessons day and night, beat him with rods, until he was bruised all over, and suffered such pain that he made his escape from the cave. But the monsters were after him across the country, over hill and dale, until he came to the top of the high mountain which overlooked the desert, and the monsters being close behind, there was nothing left for him in his last extremity but to leap for his life and liberty.

And Noel Biffin did leap; but instead of being dashed to pieces, the Dunce came down from his perch on the stool to the floor of the schoolroom, the noise of which roused the usher from his nap, who gave the stupid boy a dose of cane pie and sent him home.

## "I DON'T KNOW."

OUR little hero lived in a very pretty cottage on the hills. He was fond of reading, and his parents, who could well afford it, indulged the boy to his heart's content with interesting books.

By his schoolmates this lad was known by the nickname of "Careless Harry," because he was so untidy and negligent in his habits. Out of all the expensive books that had been purchased for him there wasn't one that had a decent cover. Indeed, some of them had their backs completely broken with ill-usage, while others hadn't a back at all. Besides being careless and forgetful the boy had still another fault. If his mother asked him a question, the answer was sure to be, "I don't know."

"Where's your hat, Harry?"

"I don't know."

"What have you done with your ball?"

"I don't know."

"Child, however did you tear your clothing in that frightful manner?"

"I am sure I don't know."

His room was littered with his books, toys, and playthings. There stood the rocking-horse with his tail pulled out. Here, flat on its back, lay his sister's big doll, its poor face dreadfully disfigured by Harry's mischievous fingers. His mother was very much displeased with him, and had sent him to bed, promising to take severe measures with him if she ever heard "I don't know" from his lips again.

Harry was very frightened. He did not wish to vex his mother, or to act unkindly towards his sister, and so, resolving to be more careful in the future, he covered his head over with the bed-clothes and fell fast asleep.

But Harry's carelessness had raised the ire of others besides his mother and sister, and they were determined to punish him.

It is all very well to treat books, dolls, drums, rocking-horses, and other playthings as if they had no life in them, but careless boys may do that once too often. So it appeared in this case. Harry was no sooner asleep than these ill-fated creatures held a great discussion with reference to his cruelty.

"I'll not stand this any longer," cried Robinson Crusoe, stepping from the boy's bookshelf. "I'm getting an old man, and I won't be insulted by having my only covering torn from my back by this young rogue. There he is covered up quite snug, while I am standing here shivering in my shirt."

"And I," responded little Red Riding Hood, "would gladly see him punished. He has thrown so much soapy water over me I feel as if I'd been shipwrecked in the washing-tub."

"And I," echoed the Drum, "owe him a grudge, not so much for the hard thumps he has bestowed on my person, as for his disgraceful treatment of yonder fair lady, whose dear nose he has completely put out of joint. That lady doll is my relation. We were born in the same place, were sent out in the same ship to Australia, and have occupied the same shop, until purchased and brought here to be cuffed and ill-treated by this boy. Gentlemen, I mean to avenge the lady."

Now the ice was broken, accusations came so fast and thick against the unlucky culprit that it was quite impossible to make them all out. Fishing rods, minus line or hook, bats without handles, balls and tops, which danced like mad around the bed—the hubbub became so great the wonder is the whole house was not roused by his accusers.

The noise, however, woke Harry, who sat bolt upright in bed, and gazed with a bewildered stare at the queer crowd surrounding him. He was too much alarmed to speak, but one glance showed him Robinson Crusoe, clad in nothing but his fly-leaves, standing at his bedside, with many others, who in the dim light he could not recognise.

"Place him on my back, friends, and I'll gallop away to—'*I don't know*,'" cried out the tailless Rocking-horse in a terrible voice; and the words were no sooner uttered than poor Harry was quickly blindfolded, dragged from his bed, and placed astride the horse, who instantly galloped out into the cold night with him.

The pace at which the steed travelled was a caution. Harry had once accompanied his father to Gawler by rail, but the speed of the train was like travelling on a bullock dray in comparison to the flying pace of that beast without a tail. How he held on to its back is a positive wonder. All he saw was the clear starlit sky above his head, rocking and rolling about like the waves at the Semaphore on a windy day. His poor feet ached with the cold, for his only covering was his night-gown, and his legs felt as though they didn't belong to him. At length, just as he was beginning to feel faint and giddy from exhaustion, the Rocking-horse stopped, and the bandage was removed from his eyes. Ah! what a sight he beheld. There was the Drum he had broken strutting about on legs like a human being, who

"A JACK-IN-THE-BOX . . . CAME AND REVILED HIM."

came up to Harry with a haughty swagger, and said, "Boy, why did you break my head?"

And then a Hoop came, and demanded, "why he was thrown aside in the lumber-room?" and a black Jack-in-the-box, whose scanty locks had been wantonly torn from his scalp, came and reviled him; and, lastly, his late victim, the poor doll, made its appearance in a winding sheet, and began to reproach him for his cruelty.

The unfortunate boy seated himself on the ground and burst into tears, but the more he wept the more his tormentors jeered at him; and really the Drum and Robinson Crusoe seemed to incite the others to insult him; therefore was our poor Harry very miserable indeed. Growing tired of playing with him, or afraid of the cold wind, perhaps, his strange companions at last took their departure, and Harry was left alone.

Such companionship had been bad enough, but solitude was worse. He started up, and shouted with all his might, "Is there anybody about?" "I don't know," sighed the wind. "Which is the way home?" shouted Harry. "I don't know," chuckled the laughing jackass. "Where's my mother?" screamed the boy. "I don't know," exclaimed a 'possum and a kangaroo together. Too frightened to speak any more, Harry groped his way along in the darkness. As day dawned he came to a very high hill, and here he saw his tormentors having some rare fun. The Doll had mounted the Rocking-horse, which was galloping round and round as they do in a circus. While the Drum beat time, old Robinson Crusoe was waltzing with the Lady of the Lake; and Jack the Giant-killer played leap-frog with Mother Hubbard, Red Riding Hood and Little Jack Horner. Their merriment grew more fast and furious every moment, but the instant they espied our hero it ceased, and a deep silence fell upon them all.

"Ladies and gentlemen," cried a Pop-gun, breaking the silence, "you are aware we have refrained from doing injury to this cruel boy, through the mediation of the 'Old Woman who lived in a Shoe.' We left him in peace to make his way home, and instead of doing so he has wantonly broken in upon our secret revelry, and so has forfeited all claim to our clemency. What shall we do with him?"

"Pitch him headlong from the cliff," replied the Drum in a deep voice.

"It shall be done," responded a chorus of voices.

Poor Harry, who had not spoken hitherto, now found his voice. "No, no! Spare me, good gentlemen; spare me!" he cried.

They only mocked him for his pains. "Hearken to him pleading for mercy! Careless Harry! cruel Harry!" and amidst much noise and confusion the young mortal was carried to the apex of the steep, tall cliff, and pushed over into the yawning gulf below.

Poor Harry, half mad with terror, uttered a series of piercing shrieks as he felt himself falling—falling through the air—and called aloud for his mother to help him. Conceive his joy when he found himself in her arms, and heard her well-known voice reassuring him.

"You are safe, my boy, quite safe. What has frightened you?"

"Oh, mother! I have been taken away in the night."

"Taken away! Where?"

"To—to—'*I don't know.*'"

The mother smiled to herself as she left the room, and "Careless Harry" went out to see if the rocking-horse and the others had returned home.

# THE BANK CAT.

BECAUSE "Tent-Peg" on the Bogan isn't on the map of Australia, it must not be inferred that the little township does not exist. Indeed, any old colonist who knows his way about will tell you that the place is in the sister colony, and consists of one public-house, a blacksmith's shop, a store, a church (about the shape and size of a haystack), and a small branch bank.

The latter building presented nothing of the polish and artistic finish, or the magnificence of many of our metropolitan banks, but it was one of the most snug and cosy institutions in the whole country, within its walls. No doubt Toney Buck, the messenger, was of the same opinion, as he sat dozing before a warm coal fire, this severe winter night, with no other company than a large black cat, of the male gender, for his companion.

Toney Buck was an orphan, aged twelve years, or thereabouts, and acted in the dual *rôle* of servant to the manager and messenger to the bank. The boy slept on the premises, and the manager having gone to visit a neighbouring squatter, his servant had been ordered to sit up until he returned. There Toney sat in the manager's armchair, bowing and nodding to the fire, as if it had been some great fetish to whom he was paying homage. Toney was a very practical lad. Nothing fanciful or dreamy ever bothered Toney. Had the boy been otherwise, I'm afraid he wouldn't have had anything to do with the bank, because his employers were anything but poets or visionaries, as some of my borrowing friends can testify. However, be this as it may, every time our hero opened his heavy eyelids after each jerk forward, he encountered the round, black, winking orbs of Tabby fixed full upon his face, with a strange expression stamped thereon. Indeed, more than once Toney felt certain that the cat actually laughed at him, and when discovered in the act, instantly attempted to compose its features and wink at the fire in a knowing way. It is not a very easy task for a sleepy boy, who feels as if his eyelids were freighted with four-pound weights, to rouse himself and his waking faculties all in a moment, but Toney managed to sit bolt upright after a time and to stare at his companion. Toney fancied he could stare. So he could without a doubt; but the cat could and did stare harder than Toney. Its eyes never moved, in their fixed look, from his face, yet he could see their colour change from black to pale sea-green, and from green to grey, and then turn flaming red as the fire. Toney feeling uncomfortable, removed his chair farther back, muttering, "Oh, bother the cat!"

"Whirr. You're another," replied a voice instantly.

The messenger was in the act of sitting down again, but he gave a jump as if a snake had bitten him. He looked first at Tabby, and then at the fire bewildered, and said, "Who spoke?"

"I did," replied the cat.

"Good gracious! Are you sure now?" inquired Toney, with the scales—or the weights, rather—fallen from his eyeballs.

"I did say 'You're another'; and so you are. If you bother me I'll bother you!" replied Tabby, whisking his long tail.

"Oh, my! I never knew cats could talk, although I've heard their voices sometimes, of a night, to some tune."

"None of your sneers, Toney," interrupted Tabby quickly. "There are more wonderful things in Australia than a talking cat, and some noises to which our midnight concerts are as sweet music in comparison. Listen to me. The bank will be robbed this very night. There!"

"Talking cat—the bank robbed. I—I hope I'm awake," cried Toney, tugging at his unkempt hair in astonishment.

"I hope you are, for there are those coming who will soon arouse you," replied the cat, jumping on the back of a chair, and erecting his back in the form of a rainbow. "Hark! that noise is worse than our caterwauling. Hear them forcing in the door of the front office."

As the cat spoke there came upon their ears first a low grating noise, then followed a sound as if the heavy door of the bank had been wrenched off its hinges. "Lord help us! It's the bushrangers, and master's away. Oh! what shall I do?" and the poor boy began to cry bitterly.

"Stop crying. Wait and see!" Tabby hadn't time to say more, ere three men, with masks upon their faces, and armed with revolvers, rushed into the room.

"Hallo! only a boy here. Where's the manager?" inquired one of the robbers, grasping Toney.

"He isn't here, sir."

"Come, none o' that," cried the man gruffly.

"Tell us where he is, or I'll shove you a-top of that fire."

Toney looked at the fire, and then at the bushranger, and began to cry afresh.

"Where's the manager?"

"Gone to Mr. Hilton's, the station on the river."

"Are you certain?"

"Yes, as certain as that you will be hanged."

The man let go his hold of Toney instantly, and stared first at the cat and then at the messenger, as if he was puzzled as to which had answered him. He appeared to decide in favour of the boy, for he said hoarsely, "No cheek, my fine kiddie, or I'll roast you like a chicken. Bring the keys of the safe, quick."

"Master has them in his pocket, sir."

The robber swore a frightful oath, then held converse with his companions in an undertone. After which they produced a cord, and having tied the lad hand and foot, left him in the room with the cat, locked the door on the outside, and proceeded to ransack the bank.

Poor Toney! What could he do against three armed men? The manager, his master, had been very good to him. He was father and mother and brother and sister all in one. What would he say when he returned and found the place robbed—

the money gone? Hadn't he entrusted all the gold, and notes, and papers—worth thousands and thousands of pounds—into his (Toney's) custody, and here were villains breaking open these sacred coffers with hammer and crowbar in ruthless plunder! In his trouble, he almost wished the bushrangers would come in and roast him as they had promised to do. Even that would be preferable to facing his kind master.

"Toney. Hi, Toney!" The boy jumped. He had forgotten all about the cat.

"You were always kind to me, Toney, and I'm going to help you now."

"How can a cat help anybody?" replied poor Toney.

"Ah! but I wasn't always a cat, Toney."

"Oh, bother; I suppose you mean when you were a little kitten," muttered the boy.

"No, I don't, Toney Buck. I never was a kitten. I mean when I was a happy fairy in Elfland, before I was changed into a cat for being cruel and selfish."

"Snooks!" answered Toney sceptically.

"Who?"

"Snooks! It won't do, you know. There ain't no fairies, nor moonland, and such nonsense."

"Supposing my shape were to change again,

here under your very nose; would you believe what you saw?"

"Rather! but you can't do it, puss."

"Can't I? You shall see," replied Tabby. "Say: '*Sevle naila rtsua*' very slowly. Now!"

"'*Sevle naila rtsua*,'" cried the boy in a brisk tone; but he had no sooner uttered the words than the black cat vanished into thin air, and in its place he beheld a wee, thin, elderly gentleman dressed in hunting costume, seated astride the back of the chair, who bowed very politely and lifted his hat to the astonished messenger.

"Well I never!" cried Toney. "Who are you, pray?"

"'*Sevle naila rtsua!*'" replied the little man, laughing.

"What is '*Sevle naila rtsua*'? demanded the boy.

"Read the letters backwards and join the first two syllables together."

"Ah! A-u-s-t-r-a-l-i-a-n—E-l-v-e-s—Australian Elves, eh?"

"That's it, Toney; I'm proud to be one of them, my boy. Now I'll show you how a cat can help you out of this scrape," answered the wee man, with a smile only to be seen on the face of a fairy. "I'm going out at that broken pane in the window there, straight to Dick Holmes' stable, take out the steeplechaser 'Nightwind,' ride as fast as he can go to the junction, return with half-a-dozen troopers by a short cut, and secure these ruffians red-handed with their booty.

"Hurrah!" cried Toney in his enthusiasm.

"Hush, boy. Not so loud," said the elfin; "they may hear you. I must away on my errand quickly; yet mind, Toney, if you don't see the bank cat here again, I'm always to be found on the banks of the Bogan. Keep good heart. Good-bye."

With a hop, skip, and a jump the wee man was through the broken pane and astride the horse "Nightwind" before the boy could realise that he was alone.

Meanwhile the strong-room of the bank resounded with the heavy blows dealt by the robbers upon the solid doors of the iron safe, which for a long time withstood their utmost attempts to break it open. Poor Toney sat in fear and trembling, and counted the minutes as they fled by, listening to the noises without, and wondering if the little elfin man would really do what he promised. It seemed hardly possible that he could sit a horse at all, much less guide the crack steeplechaser "Nightwind" across country on a dark night. Nevertheless, the confident tone of the fairy before he jumped out at the window reassured him, and hope began to gather in Toney the messenger.

Alas! that hope was dispelled the next moment by a loud shout from the bushrangers, which proclaimed that the safe had yielded. Had the robbers been less intent upon the bags of gold and silver which met their gaze, it is probable they would have seen the half-dozen police-troopers who entered, carbine in hand, and surrounded them. When the ruffians did see them, however, it was too late to resist, and they were taken away out into the darkened night, some of them never to see the light of the sun again as free men.

At the trial of the bushrangers the police couldn't swear who gave the information about the bank, and I believe it remains a mystery to this day.

# GUMTREE HOLLOW.

LIKE "Ben Bolt's" mill, Allan's farm, situated by the River Torrens, had gone to decay and ruin. It was a flourishing place before the death of Peter Allan, but the farmer had been taken away, and his widow and her three children had to fight out the battle of life unaided. The property had been heavily mortgaged three years previously, and, what with unfavourable seasons and other misfortunes, the widow Allan had not been able to repay principal or interest of the money borrowed, and the creditors therefore gave the farmer's wife notice to quit.

Fortunately, Mrs. Allan had a brother who had gone to some diggings in New South Wales, and had left in charge of his sister an old hut and a patch of land known as Gumtree Hollow. In the emergency the widow determined to occupy the place until she could find a more suitable home. The Hollow consisted of about two acres of crags and stones, without sufficient soil to grow a potato in, and was distant from the farm about five miles.

On a warm afternoon, three days after the widow had received notice to leave the homestead, little Charlie Allan, the eldest boy, aged twelve, started to the hut at Gumtree Hollow with his mother's goods and chattels in the spring-cart. It had been arranged that after delivering his load the lad should return for his parent and his brother and sister. Charlie was intelligent and very kind-hearted. He had noticed his mother crying bitterly, and he had followed her into a back room where his father had died, and there putting his little arms about her neck he had tried to soothe her with many assurances that when he became a man he would work for her and buy the place back again.

Old Bob, the pony, didn't like the road to the hut, but repeatedly turned to retrace his steps every half-mile or so of the journey. Nevertheless, Charlie managed to get him there at last.

In a ravine between a natural cutting of jagged crags stood the old building, overshadowed by a gigantic tree whose wide-open trunk, hollow as a bell, had often afforded shelter to straggling picnic parties. It was a grand, old, hoary gum, knobbed and gnarled with age, and whose spreading branches formed a canopy over the dilapidated hut. One long, fork-like branch projected farther over than the rest, on the extreme end of which something perched, swaying the bough to and fro with an easy motion. Charlie, thinking it was a parrot, took up a stone for a shot; but he dropped the stone again instantly, as a voice from the tree uttered a shrill peal of laughter.

The poor lad's first thought was to take to his heels and run for it; but the voice called out in a kindly tone, "Hallo! Charlie 'avic, how are ye, Charlie Allan?"

The boy gazed upward in amazement, and beheld a wee, teeny, queer fellow, hardly six inches high, sitting astride the branch, and gazing down with a knowing look at him. The creature's dress was green; from his shapely shoes to his brimless hat, swallow-tailed coat, breeches, stockings, all were the verdant green colour.

"Who are you?" questioned Charlie, recovering from his surprise.

"Shure I'm an Irishman," cried the little fellow, at the same time springing to the ground. "A rale paddy, an' I may tell you that there isn't a fay or a gnome in South Australia that I can't leap or swim wid; do's thee hear that, 'avic?"

He was such a dwarfed miniature of a man,

and appeared such an impudent swaggerer—with his chimney-pot hat on one side of his head, and his saucy turned-up nose—that Charlie felt inclined to pick him up and cuff him soundly.

"What is your name?" asked the boy, making a sudden dive at the creature.

"McKombo," answered the sprite, dodging under Charlie's legs. "My name is McKombo; but be aisy wid ye now, an' don't be after trying to take a mane advantage of me."

"I'd scorn to do it," said Charlie, unconsciously clenching his fists. "Who are you; what are you; and what do you want?"

"Be aisy, Charlie. Arrah', don't be botherin' me wid too many questions," said McKombo. "I've tould ye I'm an Irishman. Captain Brophy imported me to the colony in a hat-box twenty years ago."

"Why, you're a fairy," suggested the lad, eyeing his strange companion askance.

"Of course I am," replied McKombo, "and I may tell you I've been waiting all this blessed day to see you."

"To see me?"

"Thrue for ye, Charlie. I am very well acquainted wid all the bother an' trouble that's going on at the farm, an' I mane to help your mother clane out of it."

Poor Charlie felt as if he could have hugged McKombo, but the sprite kept his distance and said quietly, "You haven't such a thing as a spade and a pick among the things in the cart?"

Charlie had, though. Both the pick and the spade he had used many a time at the farm, and

"'HURRAH!' HE CRIED, TOSSING UP HIS HAT."

he produced them at once; but he looked doubtfully at McKombo as to what he was to do with them or how they could be the means of assisting his mother in her difficulties. It seemed very business-like, however, the way the sprite led Charlie to the hollow trunk of the great gum-tree, and commanded him to dig within a certain circle he at once marked out. The goblin's promises of certain and speedy benefit gave the boy faith and energy to dig and delve away with might and main until there gaped a large hole within the trunk, which revealed some of the thick roots beneath, also the top of a square tin box, such as lawyers keep their deeds in. The moment McKombo caught sight of the box he began to caper about the sward in antic glee.

"Hurrah!" he cried, tossing up his hat. "There it is, me boy, safe an' sound, as on the night I saw them murthering scoundrels place it there twenty years ago."

Poor Charlie stared at the fairy, and wiped the perspiration from his heated face, but he could not comprehend what his companion meant. Acting under McKombo's directions, young Allan made a lever and got the box out of its bed. It did not appear large, but it was very heavy— so heavy that the boy could hardly lift it; the thick coating of paint on it had preserved it from rusting and decay, and it was fastened with an iron padlock. With one blow of his spade Charlie broke open the lid, when—lo! he saw a heap of dark yellow sovereigns and several parcels of banknotes within. The sight made him faint and giddy with surprise and delight, so that he could not utter a word.

"Look there, now. See that," ejaculated the sprite, pointing to the treasure. "One evening, twenty years ago, three men brought that box here and hid it beneath the trunk of this old gum-tree; they went away, but never returned for it. In time a poor woodcutter built his hut beneath the great tree, and I watched him come and go to his daily toil, until he could toil no more and they carried him forth and buried him on the river-bank. Then came your Uncle George, my boy, who purchased the place for ten pounds; but had he known of the riches under his very nose, I'll go bail he wouldn't have gone away to dig for gold."

"Why didn't you tell Uncle George about this money?" asked Charlie.

"Bekase he would have spent it recklessly, honey, that's why. Money ill-spent or mis-applied is a great evil. Put the box on the cart wid the things, and return to your mother. Off wid ye, boy, at onst."

"Won't you come with me?" pleaded Charlie.

"I can't, 'avic, I'm going to a christening at McFadden's in the Glen. Away ye go. Good-bye." Saying which, McKombo vanished from his sight.

Widow Allan was very much astonished when Charlie returned and told his story, but her surprise was still greater when she saw the box of hard cash. She counted the money, which amounted to over three thousand pounds sterling; after which she fastened the box again, and wrote a letter to the manager of a certain bank in Sydney, and to which most of the notes belonged.

In due course the bank sent a representative to Allan's farm, who informed the widow that the bank had been robbed of over three thousand pounds one night in June twenty years ago, and which had never been recovered. The bank agent departed with the money, but he left the poor but honest widow a cheque for £500—a sum which not only paid off the liability upon her farm, but enabled her to put something by for a rainy day and for Charlie when he came of age.

# WHISKERKISS.

## CHAPTER I.

### THE MYSTERIOUS JOURNEY.

IN the heart of the far Australian wild—away from traces of civilisation, and beyond the hope of help, a brave youth, faint with travel and with hunger, reclines completely exhausted by the bank of a broad river. He is the last of a band of nine who have attempted to explore the central portion of our vast continent, where on the Atlas we read, written right across the great blank, *Unexplored.* All his companions have perished of want and thirst, and Roland Trent, although he has reached water, and has quenched his burning thirst, feels that he also must follow his comrades ere long. He is very weak and so fatigued that he cannot stand; but he can see the flowing stream and the sunlit landscape, which anon becomes o'erclouded in his vicinity by the shadow of some moving object between him and the river. What could it be?

The explorer looked up in wonder, and beheld a small and very ugly old man standing and grinning at him. The creature was most outrageously grotesque in form—having, by some freak of nature, the body of a child with the head of a giant. No one, not even Mr. Punch, could boast a finer hump than protruded from between the shoulders of the intruder. From out a circular hole in his jerkin the hump rose bare, behind the big round skull, like a sugar loaf. He had small eyes, but they were infinitely more terrible than all his other deformity put together; at one moment they glowed with a phosphorescent sheen, which changed again to a vivid purple light, and from that to diamond flashes, without the closing of an eyelid.

"Ho! Ho! Who is more powerful than fire, stronger then the wind, and deeper than the streams? Whiskerkiss—I am he."

The voice of the old fellow was dreadful, and echoed with a sullen roar like the growl of a lion, " I am Whiskerkiss, King of the Mountain Barrier, and Lord of Birds and Beasts. Who art thou?"

The lips of the fainting youth answered, "An unfortunate explorer."

"Ha! Ha!" laughed the grim sprite in mimicry. "Thou puny mortal! Thou an explorer! Why, thy poor breath is nearly spent, ere thou hast reached the threshold of the great *Unknown*. Ho! Ho!"

Roland Trent shuddered.

"Wouldst thou see the wonders of this vast division of the globe? Come with Whiskerkiss, and he will show thee fertile lands, great lakes, and powerful nations in this unexplored interior. Come! here is my boat, and Starmoon, my slave, lashes the stream impatiently."

As the dwarf spoke, he lifted Roland in his arms and placed him in a skiff upon the river, which immediately shot along the watery way with the speed of an express train. It was some time before Roland Trent recovered from the half unconscious state in which he had been conveyed to the boat; by-and-by, however, his vision became more clear, and he saw a sight he had never seen before. The skiff was nothing but a frail canoe, at the stern of which stood Whiskerkiss steering; but in front, a great, strange fish was harnessed to the bow, and plunging through the stream with immense velocity.

No pearl diver ever encountered such a quaint-looking denizen of the deep, as Starmoon the goblin fish of Whiskerkiss. It was in shape like an alligator, only its legs were as those of a grasshopper, which it used in place of fins while swimming. Fully twenty feet in length, it had a body as thick as a bullock, and a long spike projecting out of the top of its head. The face of the monster was hideous to behold—the rolling eyes, dreadful mouth, filled with a row of sharp, glistening teeth, and above all, it appeared to jibber, and make faces at our hero, as he looked at it in its swift course.

And now the river widened into a deep black gulf, and the shore receded from their gaze; not a ripple broke over the sullen surface, for the waters were like thick oil. Dark objects, in rapid motion, darted along like dolphins, and played leap-frog over the skiff. Roland Trent put his hand over the side; to his astonishment the water felt quite hot. He dipped a little up in the hollow of his palm, and tasted it. Pah! It was not salt, nor fresh, but worse than either, as it instantly produced a horrible nauseous feeling in him akin to stupor.

Onward went Starmoon at increased speed, urged by his master Whiskerkiss, until Roland beheld a great mountain range in the distance, which they rapidly approached. Abrupt and perpendicular, the summit of these high hills was lost in the clouds. The canoe sped onwards, and it seemed as if the frail barque would be dashed to atoms against their rugged sides. Daylight faded away as they drew near, and a distant roaring noise shook the sluggish waters. Were they hurrying to some fatal mäelstrom, or going headlong into some tremendous cavity in the bowels of the mountains? Roland's spirit quailed within him at the thought. In the dim twilight, he saw the boat had entered an enormous cavern, where a dense wall of black rock, or rather boulders, were piled in wild disorder one above the other, and terminating in a flat roof of the same description.

"Ho, ho! I am Whiskerkiss, King of Woods and Stream," and the voice of the steersman awoke the slumbering echoes of the dreary place with ten thousand vibrations.

"Who sails through rocks and hills, and guides the torrent in its course? I, Whiskerkiss. Ho! Starmoon. Ho! my slave, delve, delve!"

Gradually the darkness became more opaque around them. Roland cast himself down at the bottom of the canoe, and awaited his fate. He closed his eyes in horror at the vision of that dread abyss.

The time passed on, and still the same ghastly darkness prevailed. Our hero knew not whether it was night or day, or how many hours had passed since they had entered that dreadful passage under the mountain. From a sort of torpor into which he had fallen Roland was at length aroused by a touch on his cheek. It was not the touch which animated him so quickly, but the intensely pleasing sensation which it caused. Like that warm, thrilling emotion caused by the infusion of laughing gas, Roland felt a vigorous glow pervade his whole frame in an instant. He opened his eyes, but the bright rush of the noon-day light which burst unexpectedly upon his sight completely blinded him.

He shaded his eyes at first, until he should become accustomed to the glare. When at length he looked up, lo! where were Starmoon and Whiskerkiss, and the black unclean waters of the murky cavern below the mountains? Gone! With his hearing more acute, his sight much keener, and with every other faculty braced and quickened, the explorer found himself the occupant of a beautiful boat canopied with gold and silver network of rare design and workmanship. The sides and bottom of the skiff were inlaid with mother-of-pearl, while a large outspread fan, at the stern, of the same material, gave the resemblance of a gorgeous peacock floating on a silver stream. A dozen creatures, dazzlingly fair, and dressed superbly, propelled the boat with ivory paddles; while one who appeared robed in roseate splendour stood at his side, and pointed out to him a glorious country.

Yonder shone an immense valley, shut in by Alpine hills, of a deep, rich green, spangled with flowers. Birds of every hue and shade flitted from tree to tree, and filled the air with melody. At the foot of the hills a clear lake sparkled in the sunlight, and beyond the lake rose the towers, peaks, and domes of a beautiful city of white marble, which flashed back the sun's rays in a million shafts of different coloured lights. The magnificence of this scene grew each moment yet more glowing and brilliant as Roland Trent gazed. Soon there smote upon his ear most ravishing sounds—sounds that seemed as the tinkle of silver bells, mingled with the soft murmurs of the Æolian harp. To his astonishment Roland discovered the melody proceeded from his companions, who were conversing with each other, and in his own language. Next to the gratification of finding himself in such an enchanting region, the explorer was delighted to find these people could understand and converse with him.

"Gentlemen," said he, bowing politely, "will you have the goodness to tell me what country this is I now gaze upon for the first time?"

The rowers ceased rowing at the sound of his voice, and the nearest to him answered,—

"O! adored mortal, we are thy slaves. This is the kingdom of Bo-Peep, and is called Dreamland. No feet of soul-lit mortal hath ever trodden our soil before. Hail to thee! immortal one!"

"Are you the King of this fair land?" inquired our hero.

"Nay, I am but his Majesty's messenger—my name is Pop-Corn. What shall we call thee?"

"Roland, the Explorer."

"Welcome, then, to our shores. Thou shalt see Bo-Peep and his daughter Princess Golden Hair."

The rowers resumed their paddles, and the fairy boat shot down the shining stream into the lovely sheen of the lake by the marble city.

Moments in Dreamland are as days with us. Therefore it will take a week of our time to prepare the charming Princess Golden Hair to receive our hero. Next Saturday the bold explorer shall be ushered into her presence at the Court of Bo-Peep.

## CHAPTER II.

### PRINCESS GOLDEN HAIR.

THE metropolis of Dreamland presented a most glorious spectacle of magnificence and beauty to the wondering eyes of Roland Trent, as the fairy boat glided into the lake near the city. Beneath a fine marble colonnade, supported by pillars of jasper, he beheld a crowd of people, composed chiefly of Ministers of State and the nobles of the King, standing ready to give him welcome, while beyond these dignitaries a great square was filled with his Majesty's Guards, armed *cap-à-pié* in silver armour, and surrounded by lithe, gay figures, who flitted to and fro like gorgeous butterflies in the sunlight.

The Australian youth was amazed at the dazzling beauty of the ladies, who gathered round him as he landed, with loud cries. Some of them even went so far out of the rule of good breeding and etiquette in their reception as to embrace and almost smother him with kisses. But there are no Mrs. Grundys in Elfland, and so the dames enjoyed themselves with the freedom and the innocence of children. With waving banners and bands of music, which sounded to his ears like so many tinkling musical boxes, our hero was escorted by a troop of silver-clad Guards to the palace of Bo-Peep. Grander than anything that ever entered the mind of that famous architect, Sir Christopher Wren, rose the glittering domes and lofty peaks of the fairy King's palace. Through a labyrinth of budding roses perfuming the air around; by gold and silver fountains in full play, and whose soft cadence fell upon the ear like angels' whispers; beneath a natural arch of mighty trees, every one of which held a thronged choir of winged choristers warbling forth a jubilee; and onward, amid glories and beauties unknown to the hosts of the waking world, into the presence of Bo-Peep. No comparison in this sea-bordered city would help to convey the faintest conception of the pomp and splendour of the King's reception-hall. Nature and Art had here combined, and the blended effect was sublime. Not the array of nobles nor the throng of superbly dressed ladies, through whom he passed, nay, not even the throne itself, ablaze with jewels and precious stones, which circled in the elfin monarch as the ring of a magic lantern, had any attraction for the young stranger. His eyes had fallen upon a young creature of enchanting loveliness at the King's side, and he had become spellbound thereby.

Poet or painter never dreamed of such a vision of beauty. Not the sunset glow had a richer tint than the long glossy hair of Bo-Peep's only daughter. She was named "Princess Golden Hair"; and well did she merit the name, for it was the most glorious golden hair that mortal eye had ever seen. So Roland Trent thought as he was led forward and seated by her side.

Here where the laws of Nature (as we recognise them) are altered and suspended, the Princess and the mortal wanderer became enamoured of each other instantly.

Oh! the power, the irresistible charm of love! How it glowed in the eyes of Princess Golden Hair, and made the bewitching face yet more charming! Like the clear notes of a flute, only infinitely softer and more thrilling, her voice came upon his ears: "Welcome, oh, my Prince—lord of my being!—welcome to Dreamland!"

What mattered the cheers of the people and the great speech from the fairy King, and the grand banquet that followed—what mattered the thousand surprises and the wonderful things that encountered him at every turn? There was no fascination like the lovely Princess.

Glorious light and sunshine reigned here eternally. Roland watched in vain for the approach of eve and darkness; but gloom came not. It was one never-ceasing day.

By order of Bo-Peep, our hero was attired in rich robes softer than silken velvet, which emitted a rose-coloured glow, mingled with a delicious

"SEATED BENEATH A CANOPY OF ROSES."

perfume, that by some mysterious power gave him a keener zest for pleasure and enjoyment. Go where he would, the King's daughter was ever at his side.

What bliss to be with her on the bright lake, seated beneath a canopy of roses in the royal barge; what sensations he felt with his head pillowed on her lap, and her snow-white fingers toying with his curls!

"The sun never fades in this enchanting valley?" he asked.

"No," she replied softly. "The great light is our life. Dulness is destruction in Dreamland. We are only creatures of an hour, that is all."

Oh, what witchery in the low, thrilling voice! Creatures of an hour, forsooth. Take care, Princess Golden hair! Take care.

"Your people are very beautiful, my Princess; but thou art fairer than a summer dream," he responded gaily.

"Flatterer, I and my people are but as dreams," she answered, smiling. "All thou see'st here of brightness and splendour are merely passing visions, nothing more."

"Thou art more real and enchanting, dear Rosebud, than any dream that has haunted me."

"Nay, adored stranger, mock me not," said Golden Hair. "I am as the wind, which fills our sail—here, there, then gone for ever. Life with me is but a breath. But thou—thou wilt live when the wind and the vast sun, which giveth our race life and motion, are fled for ever.

"Dear Princess," and he caught her hand within

his own, looking into her eyes the while, "Love is not a breath, a sunbeam. It is mightier than the wind, and more powerful than the combined forces of sea and air. Didst thou ever love, sweet maiden?"

What soft diffused light, glinting from the rich window of some ancient cathedral, ever shed such a rosy glow as was seen for one brief instant upon her face?

"Oh, Love has come with thee from beyond the Western Mountain," she answered quietly.

"And thou hast felt its presence?"

"Ay, in thee. Yet thou hast brought a demon with thee also," she replied.

"The sprite Whiskerkiss; of course, I remember."

"Nay, not Whiskerkiss; but a gnome a thousand times more terrible than the monster of the Barrier."

"And what is that, Princess?"

"Pain," replied Golden Hair.

"What! has Pain never entered into this realm?" he inquired with amazement.

"Never."

"Wonderful!" he ejaculated. "Had my charming Princess ever the toothache?"

The ringing laugh which burst from her lips was like the carol of a canary on a June morning.

"Nor the whooping-cough or—or the measles?" he added, smiling at her excessive merriment.

"Stop, stop!" she cried, looking at him with a wilful light in her large eyes, that held him as a spell. "The words thou hast uttered are unknown to me, even as Pain was unknown to me ere I saw thee."

A cloud fell over his handsome face at her words, which did not escape Golden Hair, for she added quickly, "Lord of my life, Love and Pain are twinborn, and go hand-in-hand, but the one is so beautiful that it destroys even while it creates the other. Thou seemest to me all love. Tell me, are all thy race like thee?"

"Fair Princess," he replied gravely, "beyond the Mountain Barrier from whence I came the people are as varied as the hues on yonder peak. Some there are who feel not love. Many suffer pain willingly in the service of a powerful world-god called *Money*. Amid the many fetishes who are honoured and exalted, none are more esteemed than this. At his word mighty empires rise in the wilderness, oceans are bridged, space changed into a willing slave."

"Money is a mighty demon," answered Princess Golden Hair.

"Yes, lady," continued Roland. "Money is

mighty, but ere now he has lent his power to an evil spirit called Hate, who going broadcast among the races of men has incited them to gather together and destroy each other without cause."

"Hate is a monster, uglier than Pain," replied the fairy.

"Ay, and he is invariably assisted by three other wicked powers known as Murder, Slander, and Malice."

"Poor lost people!" cried the gentle Princess. "Is there no good genii to do battle with these wicked ones?"

"Oh yes; the renowned champion Sympathy has unfurled his banner to meet the hosts of evil in the world; and by-and-by the people who have groaned groans from their birth shall live as serene and peaceful as the shadows on this lake. And now, sweet love, I would fain close my eyes in repose, under the melody of thy lute."

Sweetly fell the cadence over the still waters. Goldenly shone the domes and peaks of the marble palaces, as Roland Trent dreamed.

Shall we wake him out of his glorious vision? Nay; let him slumber on. He will open his eyes soon enough upon the realities of this sober empire at the Antipodes.

# A CROOKED SIXPENCE.

PATTER, patter, splash, splash, drip, drip, fell the rain on the housetops, down the waterspouts, and along the narrow streets of the New South Wales capital. A dismal evening to be abroad; the fierce wind playing antic tricks with the people returning home from work, by driving the rain full in their faces, turning their umbrellas inside out, and compelling many to seek temporary shelter beneath verandahs and the projecting gables of high buildings.

The tempest of wind and rain didn't appear to trouble a small, dirty-looking urchin who had taken up his quarters in a sheltered nook at the corner of one of the main thoroughfares of the city, and where he crouched, watching the vehicles, with their gleaming lamps, dash onward through the mud and wet. The poor child's clothes would have suited a warmer temperature than the keen wind and rain; but he indulged in an occasional short run beneath the portico to keep his blood in circulation. It was while taking his trot to and fro that the boy's attention was attracted by the stoppage of an omnibus, which drew close up to the curb to allow an old gentleman to alight therefrom. He was a portly old fellow, buttoned up in a portly overcoat, and he carried a portly umbrella. The boy noted this by the light of the gas lamp as the passenger went by him, and he also noted a small dark object lying on the wet pavement, not a yard away, *that was not there before.*

"Hallo! What's this? A pocket-book with money in it. That gentleman who passed has lost it. Hi, sir, hi!" And away ran the urchin in pursuit of the elderly gentleman. The little fellow overtook him, after a good chase against the pelting rain, which soaked his thin garments through and through. "I say, sir, hi!"

"Be off, boy! I never give to beggars," said the old gentleman, turning round upon the lad briskly.

"I ain't a beggar," answered the little fellow with spirit. "I ran after you to know if yer lost anything just now."

"Lost! lost! not a——I say, by Jove! you —you don't mean to——why, if it is not gone, and I would not lose it for——"

The actions of the portly gentleman were

somewhat singular. He first passed his hand hastily over the breast of his buttoned-up coat, then he threw down his open umbrella on the pavement—which the wind carried away in a moment—tore open his clothing violently, and dived into the recesses of a capacious inner pocket. Then he began a frenzied sort of war-dance in front of the boy. "I had it in my hand not ten minutes since," he cried excitedly; "and I can swear to it before the Mayor and all the J. P.'s in the colony. Mark that."

"Mark what, sir?"

"Why, I have told you—haven't I? My pocket-book, full of——Ah! I see you have found it, my good, honest lad," he went on, altering his tone, and recovering his composure as the child held out the bloated purse to its owner. "Full of documents, boy; of no use to anybody but me. Thank you for restoring it."

He snatched at the recovered treasure, and hastily unfastened the clasp to see if any of its contents had been disturbed, revealing to the youth some of the documents, which appeared marvellously like bank-notes, and a good many of them.

"It's all right, my little man. Stop! What is your name?"

"Eddy Wilkinson, sir."

"Eddy Wilkinson, eh? Where d'ye live, boy? Where's your father and mother?"

"Father's dead; and we live in Baker's Court, Redfern," answered Eddy, turning to depart.

"Stay one moment. I like to encourage honesty. Honesty is the best policy, eh?" cried the old gentleman, fumbling in his vest pocket. "Here is sixpence for you, and to-morrow, if you call at the office of Balam Bros., Woolbrokers, York Street, I will consider about a further reward. Now run off home out of the wet."

"It's very mean of him, so it is, only to give me sixpence for finding such a lot of money," muttered Eddy, as he trotted homeward through the storm. "Well, well, I must not grumble; sixpences are sixpences these 'ere times—so mother says. But what a thin, battered old coin it is!" he cried, holding it up beneath the glare of a gas lamp. "I believe it's a bad one!" and the boy closed his sharp teeth on it the next moment.

"Oh dear! Oh!" shrieked a voice, which seemed to issue out of Eddy's own mouth. The poor child dropped the coin instantly, and ran for his life; but he soon recovered from his surprise, and returned to where the sixpence lay on the shining flag in the full light of the street lamp.

"Surely it wasn't *you* who cried out just now?" said Eddy, apostrophising it.

"Yes, *it was*, and you have hurt me very much, biting me in such a savage way," replied the crooked sixpence reprovingly. "Here have I been rudely tossed and hustled from pouch to pocket, and hand to hand, to try and serve you, and you show your gratitude by saying I'm *bad*. For shame, Eddy Wilkinson."

"Indeed, I'm very sorry, ma'am," rejoined Eddy, astonished and trembling all over at the strange incident.

"I'm not of the feminine gender, Eddy. Don't call me 'ma'am,' please."

"Very well, sir," apologised the boy.

"That's worse; I'm not a gentleman."

"What are you, then?" asked the lad, in an impatient tone.

"Neither one nor the other, yet I'm a little of both. If you turn me on this side, I'm a man; roll me over, and I'm a woman. Still I'm incongruous, and only a sixpence," replied the coin.

"You're very thin, and worn, and of no earthly use to anybody, I think," said Eddy boldly, "except the banks, who are taking worn-out customers like you."

"I shall prove very useful to you, Eddy, so don't insult me. On me, thin as I am, you will build a stupendous fortune."

"Oh, let us be joyful!" cried Eddy, shaking the rain from his rags.

"And when you grow to be a man, and are elected Mayor of this city," added the sixpence, "you will wear me on your watchchain as a relic, to remind you of your first advanced step in life."

"You old humbug! I've a good mind to pick you up and spend you at the confectioner's over the way," answered Eddy, laughing.

"They won't have smooth money there," rejoined the coin. "Take my advice, and put me in your pocket out of the wet. As you said just now, I'm very thin, and I can't stand the rain."

"What shall I do with you then?"

"Put me by in that old teapot in the cupboard at home until you get another of my race to keep me company," answered the voice of the crooked sixpence earnestly. "Remember, boy, a penny saved is a penny gained, for it is by such small beginnings that people have amassed fortunes to benefit humanity, and by saving pennies and sixpences, little boys who have no fathers to work for them have been enabled to assist their widowed mothers and to make their home comfortable and happy."

"That is quite true. I'm sure, I often wish I could keep my mother, who is always working," answered the child in a sad tone.

"Your wish will be gratified, Eddy, if you only take my advice," said the voice, in the same resolute accent. "You are ten years old, and you ought to begin to earn money. The gentleman whose purse you restored wants an office boy. When he sees you to-morrow he will employ you, because the prompt manner in which you returned his pocket-book has made a good impression on him. Be careful to maintain and strengthen that effort by being trustworthy, honest, and truthful; above all, never forget the old teapot in the cupboard, where I shall be ready to welcome every new-comer placed therein."

"I'm so glad I'm going to work to help mother, and I'll not forget what you have said to me," replied the boy.

"I am fully aware of it, Eddy Wilkinson," responded the voice modestly. "I have seen a great deal of human nature in my travels, and I have noted that people—both old and young—rarely forget what I say to them. You must know that I never came out of the Mint. I was born of a good old fairy family on the Queensland border. From my childhood I hated *Money*, and was constantly railing against it and its evil influences, until our chief, Fen, transformed me into a sixpence as a penalty for my abuse of *Mammon*. In less than a month I went from the dainty purse of the Governor's lady to the dirty fob of a sweep. Once I was the only coin in the pocket of a poor solitary swagman travelling in the bush, who was attacked by a robber and foully murdered; but had you seen the murderer's face after rifling my master's pouch, and to find only me, you would have said, as I did, that crime brings its own punishment. Again, a very proud man dropped me on the pavement, and disdaining to stoop for me, there I lay for hours trampled by the crowd passing up and down. A poor, despairing, wretch, without a home, without a friend—without even the smallest means of procuring a meal—hurried with feverish haste through the by-ways of this great city, to end his life and his misery in the river; but he discovered me in his path. Weary and faint with long fasting, I supplied him with food and a night's lodging. With the return of day came other thoughts and fresh resolves, and so the man was saved the awful act of self-destruction, and lived to bless the old crooked sixpence."

And so did little Eddy Wilkinson, my dear children. The firm of "Balam Brothers & Wilkinson" is one of the most sound and thriving concerns in the colonies. The junior partner has just been elected to the civic chair of Sydney, and when he dies he intends to bequeath the crooked sixpence to the Museum.

# THE BALL IN THE DELL.

TOTTIE MAYBUSH, of Melgrove on the hills, was never known to tell an untruth. Yet little kind-hearted Tottie could not be certain whether she had fallen asleep and dreamed all about the fairies' ball, or the spirits of the dell had carried her off bodily to their annual festival. On one of our beautiful Australian midsummer nights, the dark-blue sky, and the earth beneath it, illumined by a full, radiant moon, Tottie was seated under a large fig-tree in the garden, playing with Sultan, the retriever puppy. The child's parents had gone to visit a neighbour; therefore there was no one at home save Jane, the servant, who had promised Tottie that she might remain up till they returned.

No one can say—not even Tottie herself—how it was she came to leave her seat and the puppy, and stroll all alone down the long walk beyond the orchard, until she emerged upon a sloping lawn that dipped with an easy fall to the edge of the river. The round, full moon overhead cast thin streaks and broad bars of soft light athwart the branches of the tall trees, which formed triangles, circles, and crosses, about the sombre trunks, and lay like scraps of burnished steel about her path. Out on the mossy bank the moon's focus seemed to rest on one great patch of light, whereon stood a group of small, slender, puny creatures, drawn up in two lines, like a regiment of soldiers on parade. Tiny and insignificant as they appeared, Tottie could not help observing their costumes, which were both elegant and superb. Every rich and varied flower in the botanical world of the Southern Hemisphere had lent its bloom and beauty to adorn their persons, while beyond their ranks, on the placid bosom of the river, sat six large, white swans, attached to the car of state, which glowed and sparkled under the beams of the moon like a mass of sapphires.

The moment Tottie appeared, the King of the fairies stepped forth and addressed her,—

"Mortal, you are invited to our Jubilee in the dell. Xylophagus, my Queen, has sent her barge of state, together with this gallant escort, to convey you thither. Fear not to come with us; we are your friends and your slaves for the hour. Gentlemen, let your royal barge approach."

The elfin monarch waved his hand, when instantly there arose upon the air a choral melody from the fairy boat, far surpassing the song of birds. No warbling bulbul, no melting note of dulcimer floating o'er the waters at still midnight, ever ravished the senses, or soothed with tones so liquid soft, as the strains which fell upon the ears of Tottie Maybush as she was borne aboard by the elves. They placed her on a couch of softest down, fringed by a border of wild rose leaves, and two lovely fairy ladies fanned her with perfumed fans, which not only warded off the mosquitoes, but lulled Tottie into a passive state, wherein she was utterly powerless to move or act, yet which left her sense of hearing and observation free and unfettered. What engines made of mortal hands could propel a boat so swiftly and noiselessly as those proud, vigorous swans, who glided onward down the river with the elfin barque and its freight as if the whole thing had been no heavier than a gossamer? What mortal ears could conceive from out the world of sound such enchanting harmony? It was the silvery lullaby of Fairyland, that our Australian sprites might chant to some fretful changeling they had adopted and sought to hush to sleep.

And now the view opens upon a magnificent

glade, with here and there a huge eucalyptus standing out in bold relief like a grim giant on guard. Here the elfin King and his grotesque retinue land, and escort their mortal guest across the velvet sward and through a grove of trees, which terminates in a deep dell—the scene of the fairy ball.

Upon a verdant, natural carpet, softer than velvet pile, stood two lines of young trees, from the roots of which the vines of the purple sarsaparilla had shot upward along the trunks and amongst the branches, and there bending with a graceful slope had met and entwined, and so had formed a long trellis-work roof, where the moon beamed through in twice ten thousand rays into the gallery beneath.

The elfin King conducted Tottie into this primeval hall, where Queen Xylophagus was seated with her ladies on a bank of wild violets. The child was quite bewildered at the wildly odd scene that met her gaze. The gallery was hung round with myriads of glow-worms and fire-flies, which illumined the place with a soft, subdued light, and shed a sparkling sheen on the particoloured robes of the gay creatures which moved to and fro about her. Here, as in the higher world of mortals, the ladies fanned and flirted, while the gentlemen flattered and were smilingly attentive; but there was no lurking devil behind it all with the elves. They, at least, were genuine.

"Approach, O mortal, and kiss my hand," cried the fairy Queen, rising and saluting Tottie. "In this dell thou shalt be fed on honeyed words. We will deck thee with jewels brought from hidden caves and gathered in bowers of green, where loop the clustered vines. Pure pearls of may-dew shall adorn thy fair young brow like summer's fruited gems, ripe and mellow."

Tottie tried to thank her Majesty.

"These are my ladies," continued the Queen, pointing to several lovely fays beside her. "Moppet, stand forth. This is our lady of the robes, who supplies a new dress for our person every morning."

A fair, wee creature rose from her seat and kissed Tottie.

"Moth and Poppy, two of my daughters, who are about to be married—Poppy, the youngest, to Prince Cornflower, and her sister, to the celebrated Grimalkin of the Hills," said her Majesty, introducing the members of the household. "Those three ladies in purple, who are teasing that old gentleman with the crutch, are Gloze, Geneva, and Moss, the King's first cousins—old maiden ladies who have never been married, and who delight in annoying the bachelors."

Perhaps it was fortunate for poor Tottie Maybush that a great noise at the other end of the gallery interrupted the Queen, otherwise she would probably have been smothered by the warm-hearted beings presented to her. The commotion was caused by the arrival of several ambassadors from the vast realm of Nature. Here advanced the representative of the Forest with stately dignity; then followed the Wind, whose tread shook the roof of the ball-room; and after him came a long procession of birds. The eagle headed one column, the wild turkey another, after which came parrots and plovers, quails, snipe, and magpies, while the jolliest of them all—the great kingfisher—brought up the rear. Round and round the hall they trooped until the whole host found suitable perches among the thick foliage of the trees, where they gazed down in wonder upon the throng beneath.

Amid a deep silence which had fallen upon the place the elfin King rose to his feet, and in a sharp, clear, piping tone, said, "We are all assembled; let the dance begin."

Suddenly the throng of birds struck up a wild medley of song, whereupon the fairies, bounding to their feet, began a fantastic dance around the grotto. Such a quick, changing whirl of steps and leaps and varied motions it would be difficult to conceive. Circles here, confusion there, up and down in mazes, until, the feathered band piping higher and wilder, the eye was unable to follow the labyrinth of gay creatures in their mad career. "The witches at Benevento" were as nothing compared to the furious freaks and vagaries of the elves; but in the midst of it all there was heard the booming of a bell, and—like enchantment—darkness and quiet fell upon the sylvan festivity in the twinkling of an eye.

"Tottie! Miss Tottie, do get up and come to bed!" cried Jane. "Your pa and ma have returned home!"

# ELSIE.

IF you were to search the whole of Australia you could not find a more beautiful place than "Hawthorne," the residence of little Elsie Barton Elsie's father was a merchant with plenty of money. He therefore erected a large house, a little way in the country, away from the dust and noise of the city. The building stood on a lofty hill, surrounded by trees and a lovely garden, with a broad river flowing down below among crags and thick foliage, and where the water seemed like a great mirror fixed in an emerald frame. Little Elsie loved music, and was always ready every morning to begin her music lessons without being scolded and driven to them, as some disobedient and naughty girls and boys are. It was a bright morning, and Elsie raised up the window to admit the fresh breeze and the sunshine, and then sat down to the piano. She had scarcely touched the keys, however, when she was startled at hearing some one pronounce her name. The voice which

Elsie heard calling her was not a gruff or a rough voice by any means, neither was it shrill or disagreeable in its tone; yet it was decidedly unlike any other voice she had ever heard before. It seemed more like the tinkling of a tiny silver bell than anything else, save that the utterance was clear and decided, and sent a thrill, half of fear, half of surprise, through the frame of the listener.

"Elsie—Elsie Barton!" repeated the voice.

Elsie turned about quickly, and stood amazed to observe upon the toilet-table near the window the tiniest and most grotesque creature in the world. The form was that of an old woman. Such a wee, graceful old lady, with a lithe, slight figure, no higher than the bottle of perfume near her. She was attired in a purple robe, green baize shoes, and a shining cloak of the same colour, with a hood attached, but which she had thrown back, disclosing her yellow hair. She supported herself with a crutch stick, about the size of a wax match.

"Well, my dear, you are no doubt astonished at seeing *me*?" said the old lady, leaning on her staff, and looking at Elsie with a smile. "Pray take out those horrid long spikes you call pins from the pincushion, and I will sit down and rest myself, for I am really tired."

There was nothing at all repulsive in the manner

or the aspect of this strange visitor. So little Elsie, overcoming her wonder and amazement, prepared the pincushion and seated the old lady thereon, then inquired in a respectful tone how she came into the room.

"'PRAY TAKE OUT THOSE HORRID LONG SPIKES.'"

"Through the window, of course, my dear," answered the creature, smiling. "We fairies come and go at divers times and seasons, and exactly how and when we please."

"Are you a fairy—a real fairy?" cried Elsie,

approaching and gazing with deep interest on the little lady before her.

"Certainly, child. Couldn't you see that? We Australian elves are not so tall as our kindred over the ocean, but we *are* fairies notwithstanding."

"I—I have read of the fairies," said Elsie shyly, "but I have never seen any of them before."

"Oh, my dear, it's a great favour for any mortal to see us. It is only good children who have the privilege. Do you know why I came here this morning?" said the old lady, fanning herself with a rose-leaf.

"No. Pray tell me."

"A poor little boy, who has been dreadfully hurt, and who lives in the little hut near the quarry, sent me to you," replied the fairy.

"Is it little Harry, the widow's boy?"

"The same, my dear."

"I will go this moment," she replied; and running down the stairs, Elsie took her sun-bonnet from the rack in the hall, and joined the elfin in the garden. Without speaking another word the fairy led the way down the hill, and away along the sunny banks of the river, and onward to a secluded dell, where Nature had exhausted the skill of simplicity. The earth undulating into tiny hillocks, was clothed with a tender verdure as soft and green as moss. The deep blue waters rolled by with a hushed ripple, that was more soothing than silence, and a blueness that rivalled the deep azure of the skies. On one side rose great masses of rugged rocks, and these and all the trees around were draped with great masses of clematis. From the roots of these there crept along the ground the beautiful vines of the purple sarsaparilla, and the grass all around was gemmed with wild violets and the blossoms of a delicately pencilled little wild orchid. The scent of the clematis made the air heavy with perfume, and the song of birds came with added music from the other side of the stream.

In this pleasant spot were gathered together a troop of elves—little, transparent people, dressed in scarlet, and blue, and amber, others in white, shining robes, and with green jewels and wreaths decking their golden curls.

Elsie Barton stood spellbound with amazement at the wonderful sight before her. Many a time she had strolled through the lovely dell previously, but she had never met either fay or sprite. While she stood with mouth agape, the old lady fairy whispered in her ear and led the child away out of the glen and over the river, where the blue smoke from the cottage wherein lay the sick boy could be seen ascending in a thin, spiral column up toward heaven, as if bridging the void between the suffering child and the ministering angels of God.

Within sight of the hut, the fairy halted, and seating herself upon a mushroom, said in a sweet, piping tone: "I cannot venture farther, Elsie. We elves are but the emblem of good thoughts and benevolent deeds. Whoever thinks least of self can see us palpably everywhere, because we are beneficence personified. Wherever there may be an act of kindness to be done, we seek out the kindly disposed to do it; but it is death to us to look upon any other mortals, save the humane and kindly hearted. Bend down, my dear, so that I may kiss you. Now, good-bye," and the tiny lady vanished in a moment.

It was a very rude dwelling built of slabs, and almost devoid of furniture, and little Elsie Barton's eyes filled with tears as she entered it and beheld on a bed, in one corner of the room, a boy about her own age, lying pale and ill. The poor lad had been obliged to work in a quarry, to help his widowed mother and his two little brothers, and a large stone had fallen down and had crushed one of his legs dreadfully. The brave child was sinking fast for want of generous diet and such nourishment as the widow was unable to procure for him, and so the fairy had brought kind-hearted little Elsie Barton to visit him ; and Elsie helped the widow to make the sick-room more light and cosy, then went home and told her mother about the sick boy ; and Mrs. Barton, after filling a basket with nice food, returned with Elsie to the cottage.

And every day for weeks Elsie Barton carried her basket of flowers and fruit, and choice morsels of dainty food for the little sufferer, until the lad grew well and strong again ; and sometimes, sitting in the small country church on Sundays, the quarry boy sees her in the family pew listening with upturned face to the preacher, while through the stained windows gleam broad bars of rich and gorgeous light, which float about her as a gossamer, and surround the gentle face as with a glory tint.

# THE WISHING-CAP.

## CHAPTER I.

A FAIR-HAIRED, freckled boy was Johnny Grudge. He was the grandson of old Grudge the wood-carter, who occupied a hut on a Government grant some few miles out of Sydney. Johnny's father and mother were both dead and buried, therefore the boy lived with his grandfather, and assisted the old man in his business.

As our hero jouneyed to the market with his wood, he often met young Master Woolcrop riding by on his milk-white pony, with a tall groom following on a fine charger, standing I don't know how many hands high; and I am sorry to say our little hero grew very envious; for, be it known, young Woolcrop's father was one of the richest men in New South Wales, while Johnny's grandfather had not enough cash to purchase a set of harness for the old mare.

"Why was I not born to have a white pony

and a servant following me?" grumbled the youth, lashing the bushes with his whip in a savage way. "I'm quite as good as he is, and bigger and stronger. Who is he to ride while I have to walk in the dust and heat? Ah, I wish—but what's the use of wishing, I should like to know? I'm always wishing for something or other, and I never get what I wish for. Now if I could only come across the elves that grandad talks about, I'd ask them for a *wishing-cap*. Then I could have all I want." And there Johnny paused and fell into a reverie, which lasted until he reached the wood market with his team.

Often during the long winter nights the old wood-cutter had talked to his grandson of the fairies, the good little people, light as the thistle-down, and beautiful as innocence, dwelling in the bell flowers, drinking the dew for nectar, and happy, ay, as happy as the moonlight night was long. Not far from the hut there were several mossy ridges where, it was said, the elves danced at night and made merry.

The boy had wished to see them. How high were they? About as tall as a sugar-stick? Why, he had an idea that it would be quite easy to capture a whole army of them, and take them home as securely as blackfish out of the creek.

Returning home, Johnny again met the son of Sir Anthony Woolcrop with a little lady by his side, mounted on a cream-coloured pony. And the little wood-carter agreed within himself that it was a shame, and resolved to seek out the fairies that very night.

So, in not the very best of tempers, and the very lowest of spirits, our hero went out to the moss ridges to seek the wishing-cap. He lay down on the soft green carpet, and kept very quiet until he heard the great clock at the post-office boom twelve; then he heard a rustle and a bustle, and voices—not so loud as the buzz of a blue-bottle, and laughter scarcely so distinct as the chirp-chirp of a canary; but he knew it was the elves, and his heart went thump! thump!

Presently he ventured to look round him. The moon was shining—as it only can shine in Australia—and by its light he saw the gayest company of miniature beings you can possibly imagine dancing merrily. Time would fail to tell you how beautiful they all were, how gaily dressed, how courteous to each other, and how graceful in every motion. Johnny rubbed his hands and fancied he was dreaming; he stretched out his hand and ran it into a lot of prickles, and that quite convinced him he was wide awake. The pain caused him to cry out, and instantly the ball became a rout. The fairies fled in great haste, some hiding themselves in the cracks and fissures of the ridges, some burying themselves under the fallen leaves, all escaping save one, and he got his feet entangled

'THE FAIRIES FLED IN GREAT HASTE.'

in a large ant-hole, and could do nothing but wriggle and cry out.

Johnny Grudge rose to his feet, and hastened to the rescue; yet when he beheld the wee creature our hero stood quite still and did not attempt to help him.

"Pray assist me out of this nasty hole; the ants are beginning to bite me," quoth the fairy.

"Certainly I will," cried Johnny; "but if I help you I want you to give me something in return."

"What will you have?" said the little fay. "Speak quickly, and get me out of this horrible web."

"I should like the wishing-cap," replied our hero boldly.

"The wishing-cap? Silly boy! Why do you ask such a boon?"

"Because I want to be as well off as young Bertie Woolcrop, who rides on a white pony with a groom following him," answered Johnny.

"Tush!" responded the fairy. "You are much better as you are."

"Am I?" said the boy in a gruff tone. "If you say that you know nothing about it, and you may stop in that hole until the ants sting you to death, before I'll help you, now! Why should *he* have a pony, and a servant, and a little girl to ride with him and to keep him company, while I——"

"You are a strong, healthy little boy, without a care," interrupted the entrapped elfin.

"I am worn with care and with hard work," answered the youngster. "My grandfather is cross; the damper is tough, and not too much of it; my clothes are worn, and my boots are gaping at the toes; the old mare is lazy, and firewood cheap. Come, what will you do for me?"

"If I gave you the wishing-cap, what would you do?" inquired the fay.

"I'd change places with the boy who rides the white pony," he answered readily.

"Very well. Be it so. Lift me out of the hole."

When Johnny Grudge raised the elfin from his awkward position, the creature commanded him to lie down on the moss and close his eyes. Our hero obeyed, and strange to relate, in a twinkling, the moonlight, grassy dell, fairy, all faded away, and he was sleeping on a soft, rich couch. He awoke with a start, and looked round him in surprise. The grey light of the morning was stealing into the room, and he saw that the apartment was handsomely furnished. A clock struck five.

At that moment the door opened, and a man in a striped jacket came in, and wished him "Good-morning." He was rather astonished when the man lifted him out of bed, took off his night clothes, and plunged him into a cold bath. It was in vain Johnny gasped, and spluttered, and protested that he didn't like it, and was not used to it. The man only shook his head very gravely, and went on plunging him till he was satisfied; then he rubbed him dry with a rough towel. After this he helped him to dress, and poor little Grudge never had so much trouble before. It occupied nearly an hour, and when it was over there was a tap at the door, and a message to say that Mr. Cramwell was expecting Master Bertrand in the study.

"Who is he?" inquired Johnny.

"Your tutor, sir, of course."

"What does he want with me?"

"To prepare you for the day's exercises," replied the servant, with a stare.

"Oh! I can get exercise enough without him," cried the boy. "Just you give me a piece of fresh damper and some tea, and then I'm off down to the creek to look for the old mare."

The man in the striped jacket held up his hands in dismay. He assured our hero the thing was impossible, and without further parley led him out of the room and down a broad, winding, carpeted stair, on which beautiful busts of ladies and gentlemen stood staring at him in wonder to see him there, and appearing as if they were about to call out to the whole household and proclaim that he was only Johnny Grudge the wood-carter.

Down at the bottom of the stairway there stood a very prim old lady in cap and apron, and looking as cold and stiff as the statues up above. Our hero, not altogether liking the severe look upon her face, attempted to push by in haste; but the dame bade the man return with "Master Bertie," and the mandate being obeyed, she turned upon the youth, and inquired if he had left his manners behind him.

"Say, 'Good-morning, Aunt Dora,'" whispered the servant in his ear, and the boy having complied, he was conducted into a chamber with more books in it than Johnny supposed could ever have been written or printed in the world.

## CHAPTER II.

THE tutor was a stern-looking gentleman in a suit of sombre tweed. He bade our hero, "Good-morning," and then began to scold him for being late; there were Latin, English, and mathematical exercises to be gone through, and they would occupy much time. With a failing heart Johnny

Grudge took up his book and looked at the page. Strangely enough to himself he could read it, and when Mr. Cramwell questioned him about it he could repeat it; but it made his head ache, and he felt sick and weary.

"If you please, may I have a little milk?" he asked; "or a little tea and jam——"

"Certainly not," interrupted the tutor. "It is time, however, that you took your tonic."

In answer to Mr. Cramwell's summons, the man in the striped jacket appeared with a wineglassful of—oh, such nasty stuff! and Johnny was obliged to take it, every drop. Feeling very much the worse for his draught, the poor boy went on with his lessons till half-past seven, when his tutor in a terrible, frigid manner said, "Master Bertrand, it is the hour for your constitutional promenade."

Johnny Grudge at first thought he was going to have a dose of something more nasty than had been given him before, but he soon learned that he was to accompany his teacher for a stroll in the gardens, and for this he was very glad; they were very beautiful—such beds of flowers, round, diamond, heart, and all sort of shapes, screened from the sun by grand, tall trees, whose leafy luxuriance formed natural groves where the birds perched and sang, to the soft music of a large fountain which splashed and flashed in millions of tiny jets.

Johnny's first impulse was to dash off at a run when he found himself in the sunshine, but he was sharply rebuked by Mr. Cramwell for his "unpardonable vulgarity," and forced to walk as solemnly as a mute at a funeral.

When the breakfast bell began to ring our little hero took courage at the thoughts of the wonderfully nice things there would be to eat. Visions of cold wild-duck, ham, pie, eggs, salmon, and jam, flitted before him; but, alas! he was wofully mistaken. All these things and more were on the table; but not for him. He had a bowl of bread and milk and nothing else, on account of his weak digestion. After breakfast there were more hard, dry lessons, accompanied by much severe rebuke, which made the time very dreary indeed. There was a French master, and a dancing master, and a fencing master, who hurt poor Johnny very much, because he couldn't keep his right elbow in a line with his wrist during the exercise. Ere dinner-time came our hero's head was ready to crack: it seemed to him to be made up of plates of red-hot iron welded together with boiling lead.

Dinner! Only one dish—roast mutton, a piece of stale bread and a glass of water! Oh, how the young wood-cutter yearned for a slice of damper, mounted with a hunk of corned beef and an onion!

After dinner came the music master, and several other masters, and after that the white pony. But by this time Johnny was so sick and tired he begged hard that he might be allowed to go to bed. Mr. Cramwell would not hear of it. So the boy mounted the white pony he had coveted, saw a little girl, as weary as himself, on a cream-coloured pony, was escorted by the tall groom in livery astride a high steed, and felt most miserable.

As the lad rode on the highway where he was wont to journey with the old mare and dray, he saw his own very self, whistling and cracking his whip, and looking as happy as ever boy looked who had the sense to be contented with health and strength. What would he not have given to jump off the pony's back and be himself again! Oh, but he couldn't do that! He had longed for the "wishing-cap," and now he had it he must wear it!

As he rode onward he began to grumble and mutter as he had done before: "Why should

I be shut up in a big house, and made to do this, that, and the other? Oh, I wish——"

He was going to wish that he was at home again with his grandfather; but he held his peace, and rode on with the little lady.

Returning to the mansion he was ushered into a state-room, where a lot of gentlemen in white waistcoats were eating fruit and drinking wine.

He had to stop there for about half an hour without speaking a word, and was regaled with one small bunch of grapes. At the end of that time he was taken away by the tutor, in whose presence he partook of a cup of milk and water with a piece of dry toast. Then he was sent to bed, as miserable as a bandicoot. In his sleep the fairy came to him once more.

"Mortal child," he cried in his ears, "are you satisfied with the change in your life?"

"No, no, good fairy," replied the sleeper faintly. "Take back the wishing-cap—let me be my own self again. Do, do!"

"Reflect, Johnny Grudge. You will have to work again, and wear poor clothing."

"I don't mind that now," replied Johnny.

"And drive the old mare to market in the heat and dust," continued the elfin.

"Send me back to grandfather and the old

mare," he cried pleadingly, "and you shall see I will never grumble again."

"Are you sure?"

"Please try me, good fay."

"But what about the white pony?"

"Bother the pony! I don't want it."

"And the tall groom?"

"He is a cruel fellow, and I never want to see him again, nor Mr. Cramwell either. Let me be myself again, dear fay! dear, kind fairy! Pray take me home again to good old grandad," and the poor dreamer began to sob in his sleep.

"Enough," responded the wee spirit in a kind tone. "The wishing-cap I will take again, and you shall return to your home and to your daily toil. Yet remember, boy, you shall resume your place here the moment you begin to grow dissatisfied. Let this lesson cure you of envy. People who ride white ponies, the same as those who ride in carriages, are no more exempt from care, toil, denial, and suffering than yourself. Learn contentment. It is a rare jewel, and better than fine clothing and white ponies. Ta-ta, Johnny."

Poor little envious boy! The bitter disappointment he felt at finding out the truth of the old adage, "All that glitters is not gold," was very keen in his heart. Yet the lesson had done him good, by showing him that we should be very miserable if we only had everything we wished for.

When the boy woke he found himself in his own poor crib within the hut; but Johnny felt very glad he was there. He rather surprised his grandfather by the willing manner in which he began to prepare for breakfast. And then he started off to look for the old mare. How light-hearted and free he felt, as he bounded away, a hop, skip, and a jump over the dewy grass, where the sun's beams glinted as on a sea of gems!

The old horse felt amazed at the way Johnny caressed her and rubbed his cheek athwart her Roman nose. And indeed the boy felt as much amazed as any of them, and vowed to himself never to be discontented again; and Johnny Grudge kept his word.

## TWO GIANTS.

THE Blue Mountains of our neighbour New South Wales, are, it has been said, the metropolis of Elfland. On those grand cliffs are caves where grim giants lie in wait ready to be summoned by the fathers and mothers of naughty, disobedient children. Away down in the cool dells the fairies hold their councils and their balls, and many a merry frolic have they when the ghosts are asleep and snoring.

I am going to tell you about giants in this story—about two giants, one called Fog, and the other named Duty, and when the tale is finished, you shall tell me which of the giants you like best.

In one of the most lonesome valleys among the mountains lived Harry Podder, a little boy whose father was a poor selector. The selector, his wife, and their only child, were quite alone in their solitude; the dell which they occupied was shut in by high, rugged cliffs, upon whose steep sides grew dwarfed gum-trees, whose outstretched limbs appeared like the expanded wings of gigantic birds of prey, ready to swoop down upon the frail bark-dwelling beneath. Wild, weird, and fantastic was the scene. Here there was no school for Harry to go to, nor neighbours' children for him to play with. The mother would take him out among the peaks and turrets, and teach him from the open page of Nature around them, until the mind of the lad became almost as strange and wild as his surroundings.

Many a wondrous tale did the fond parent invent as to what the torrent cried in its rushing, headlong course down the mountain side; and what the trees said, as they bent and whispered one to the other in the breeze; and where the clouds were going, and why the thick mists came to kill the flowers and enfold the highest spurs as with a winding sheet. Thus they were a poor but a very happy family.

But a dreadful winter came, which laid the selector on a bed of sickness, and he was very ill indeed. "Harry, my little son," said his mother, "you must go to Ridgeford for the doctor."

Ridgeford, the nearest township, was four miles distant, over a rough track across the hills, where lived the only medical man on the range. The boy hung his head, and she had to repeat her injunction.

"Ridgeford, mother! I can't go. I'm afraid."

"Afraid, Harry? Afraid of what?"

"Of the giants, mother."

"Giants, boy? Why, there are no such beings as giants."

"Oh, mother, but there is. Did you not show me the Giant Fog, that haunts our valley? Why, you and I have watched him take all kind of shapes to hide the sheep from us. He it was who led father into the river, and caused poor old 'Possum' here to fall from the cliff."

"Possum" was a large kangaroo hound, who looked up into his young master's face as his name was mentioned, and then began to frisk about him.

The mother appeared puzzled for a moment, and then said quietly,—

"Yes, I remember Giant Fog; but, Harry, I know a giant far more powerful than he. Go to the settlement for the doctor, and I will give you a letter to my giant, and he will surely help you even if Fog were to meet you on the way."

So the mother took a sheet of paper and printed on it in large letters such as Harry could read, "DUTY."

Then she wrapped up the boy as warmly as she could, gave him a note for the doctor, and pinned the message to her giant on his breast. That done, she called "Possum," the kangaroo hound, and bade him accompany his master.

Little Harry and the dog started off on their errand, while the woman attended to her sick husband. Towards afternoon a thick fog settled on the mountains, and the mother was heard to mutter, "Giant Fog will overtake my poor child, I fear."

Many times did she go to the windows and look forth in the hope of seeing him and his faithful companion descending the cliff, but each time she was disappointed.

And where was our hero all this time? Such a road as that poor boy had to travel few little boys have ever seen, much less had to traverse alone.

Harry thought little of the road; he walked along bravely, quite proud of his journey, and, above all, his message to the Giant Duty. As he and Possum climbed the hill-side and looked down on many a rugged slope, he almost laughed and said, "I wonder if there are really such things as giants in the mountains after all?"

Arrived at the township the boy gave the letter

to the doctor, who ordered some dinner for Harry, then started him and the dog homeward.

"I hope Giant Fog won't catch us here, Possum," cried the youngster, as he mounted the steep crags above Ridgeford in safety. But the words were

"BOTH HE AND THE DOG WERE ENVELOPED IN A DEEP MIST."

hardly out of his mouth when both he and the dog were enveloped in a deep mist, whirling and eddying round, till the child was quite giddy and terrified. He put his hand to his breast, pressed the talisman his mother had given him, and cried out, "Duty!" Strange, Giant Fog seemed to clear out of the way for a moment, and they stumbled onward down the crest of the mountain; but it soon became evident to Harry that all shadow of the path was lost. Still the brave boy pursued his way, and when his spirits flagged and the dog whined he cried out, "Duty, Possum, Duty!"

At length they emerged out upon a ledge of ridges with deep ravines intervening. Below the fog looked inky black.

Our hero paused, and Possum rubbed himself against him and looked up whimpering in his face. "Never mind, old boy," said Harry. "Even if this is the very castle of Giant Fog, we have Duty with us. On, Possum, on."

The kangaroo hound drew back. The boy pressed forward, and in a moment he felt he was falling rapidly through the air.

How long poor Harry lay at the base of those cruel crags he could not say, but when he recovered consciousness the dog's cold nose was against his cheek. When he attempted to rise from the ground he found one of his little arms hung useless at his side and sharp pains darted through every limb. The tears started to his eyes, for he was but a little fellow.

"Giant Fog has done us a bad turn, Possum;

yet Giant Duty will help us all right," he muttered, and fell back with a groan of pain.

The dark night fell o'er the mountains. Patiently the mother waited and watched for the return of her son. In her anxiety she was about to issue forth in quest of him when the doctor made his appearance.

"Where is Harry?" he inquired eagerly.

"Not come back yet."

"No, I made all haste to overtake him, but the fog is so thick I have missed him on the way."

While they were talking Possum dashed into the house, and without more ado began to tug at the dress of the woman with might and main, and with whines and barkings asked as plain as dog could ask for them to follow him.

The woman understood the mute appeal. Accompanied by the doctor they hastened after Possum, who led them over spurs and ridges to where lay his insensible boy-master.

Tenderly did the kind doctor lift the exhausted child, skilfully did he treat him, and faithfully did the mother nurse and tend him; but for weeks it was doubtful who was to have the victory —the good or the bad giant.

But at last one day Harry opened his eyes and

said, "Mother, I hope the doctor came and made father well again?"

"Yes, my darling, the doctor has cured father."

"I'm so glad, mother. Giant Fog was very cruel, but Giant Duty brought me home to you in spite of him; so if the doctor has made father well, it's all right. Ah! Possum. Here, Possum, old boy!"

# MOTHLAND.

## CHAPTER I.

TAKE your places. Turn down the lights. We are going to open our magic lantern once more. Ho Presto! Here we are in Victoria.

Picture to yourself a plainly furnished room in a farmhouse on the banks of the Murray River. Besides the ordinary tables, chairs, pictures, and other things you will observe a clock on the mantel-shelf over the fireplace. Now this clock is going to form the pivot upon which our story turns.

The door of this apartment was gently opened, and two children—a boy and a girl—entered. They had just stolen away unknown to the nurse, and had come here to amuse themselves. There was, however, very little in that room to amuse them. Neither hoop nor ball nor doll was here; but there was the clock ticking away like a cricket who had lost its mother. They say that curiosity is much stronger in the female, be it child or adult, than in the male portion of humanity, so the little girl drew a chair to the fireplace, and on the top of it she placed a stool, and then both the children mounted and stood face to face with the clock.

They examined the polished wooden case, and the marble base, the figures and the painted scroll work which adorned its face, then the minute-hand which they could see moving, and listened to the "Tick, tick, tick," which seemed to come from some voice within it. "Tick-tick," cried the clock, and still as the little boy looked and listened it went on without stopping, "Tick, tick, tick."

"What can it be?" said the little girl. "Where can the noise come from, Teddy?"

"Oh!" answered Teddy, "it comes from the wee fellow inside there; can't you see him moving his arm about, eh, Lily?"

Lily looked and discovered a door. "It comes from here," she said. "I should like to open it and let the old man out."

"No, no," cried Teddy, "we must not. Papa would be angry. Come away back again to nurse." But Lily poked about with her fingers, unknowingly touched a spring, and the door flew open.

There they saw a wonderful sight. There were

wheels moving round and round, and the inside shone like gold, and there was a long piece of steel hanging down like a tail, which moved from side to side, and the timepiece said louder than ever, "Tick, tick, tick."

Lily put in her finger and touched the golden inside, and still the clock ticked on. Then she touched the pendulum, and though the clock paused for a moment as if to take breath, it went on again fresher than ever, "Tick, tick, tick."

But at last she happened to poke her finger between the spokes of the little wheel, and the timepiece stopped. Lily thought it would tick again in a minute, but she was disappointed. She touched the pendulum, she touched the wheel, she touched every part; yet all to no purpose. And then the boy, Teddy, tried his hand in vain. The clock wouldn't say "Tick, tick" any more.

What was to be done?

They were very much frightened. They closed the clock door as quickly as possible, got down from the chair, put the things all tidy, and left the room.

Nothing more occurred till breakfast-time next morning, when the father called out suddenly, "Why, the clock has stopped!" and when he examined it he found the mainspring was broken.

"Somebody has been playing with the clock. Did you touch it, Teddy?"

"No, I never," answered the boy.

"Was it you, Lily?"

Now, Lily was not in the habit of being untruthful; but she was frightened and replied, "No."

"One of you must have done it yesterday. Jane saw you coming out of the room," continued the father.

By dint of questioning, Lily and Teddy at length acknowledged they had been in the room, and then the boy said Lily had touched the timepiece, and then the girl said so had Teddy; but which of them it was that had really broken the spring their father could not discover.

"Very well, my children," he said. "If you will not tell me who broke the clock, you will be punished some day." And the father spoke truly.

In that part of the Murray district where Lily and Teddy lived there dwelt a small native race of people called "Moths." This diminutive tribe lived alone by themselves in a grand shaded valley by the river-bank. They used to be seen very often by the settlers and bushmen riding home late on moonlight nights. Indeed, many travellers had stated they had seen them dancing on the green, making merry, courting, laughing, etc., while others vouched to having spoken to the creatures. Be that as it may, the Moths were there in the valley by the river, and had been there long before Teddy and Lily's grandfather first took up the splendid selection adjacent.

The wee people had taken an interest in the fortunes of the different families round about for many years, always patronising and favouring good boys and girls, and always punishing the bad ones in some form or other.

Just below the bush paddock where the valley dips down to the water could be seen a circle of emerald green, on which the Moths assembled every night when the moon shone. It was not often crossed by the feet of mortals; but any one passing that way by daylight might observe small round rings here and there, much greener than the grass around. These were Moth circles.

Here the Moths sat in little circles on raised benches made of grass blades, whilst others danced before them in the middle of the ring to music played on flutes made from the backbones of locusts.

On the night after the clock had been broken the Moths met to hold a great council. The whole race assembled on this occasion. There was the King wearing a golden crown of flowers, and the Queen decked with diamonds of dew, and all the Princes and Princesses in robes of mingled green and blue. When the council were assembled the monarch spoke thus:

"People of Mothland, you all know what an interest we take in the family near our valley, and especially in little Lily and Teddy. Now I grieve to tell you these children have been very naughty. Indeed, one of them has told a deliberate falsehood, a sin we hate and abhor beyond all things. The boy is not so guilty as his sister; it was not he, certainly, who spoilt the clock, but still he went up on the chair and looked at it; and he ought to have told this like a brave boy, instead of holding his tongue like a coward. But Lily has told a decided lie, and she must be punished. What shall we do to her?"

"Carry her away from her home, and put Scarlet Mantle in her place," said the Queen of the Moths.

"It shall be done," replied the King.

That night when Lily was sleeping soundly in her soft, pleasant bed, the King of the Moths, accompanied by some of the strongest men in his tribe, carried her away into the valley of Mothland, and they substituted Scarlet Mantle in her stead.

Jane, the nurse, took her accustomed peep into

the child's bedroom, ere retiring for the night, and was somewhat astonished to observe that her charge appeared thinner and smaller and sharper than usual.

"I suppose it's only my fancy," cried the girl; so, kissing the *supposed* child, she went her way, and left the Moth snugly coiled in little Lily's bed.

## CHAPTER II.

THE morning following the night on which the Moths took Lily away dawned brightly. The farmer and his wife fancied somehow that their little girl looked rather pale and thin; the mother thought poor Lily was ill; the father thought she was sorry for saying she didn't break the clock. But the Moths are very clever people, and of course had contrived to make Scarlet Mantle look as like Lily as possible. So she took up the child's place in the house, and ate bread and butter, pudding, lollies, wore the girl's new clothes, and was much happier than she had ever been in Mothland. One or two little things Scarlet Mantle could not entirely forget; still, on the whole, she managed to conduct herself as a civilised human child should.

But where was Lily? She was away in the

dells with the Moths, and very unhappy. Firstly, she was very tired; secondly, she was hungry; and thirdly, she was made ridiculous. These things were most tantalising, and she was ready to cry her eyes out. No wonder she was tired, because instead of going to bed at seven o'clock, and sleeping soundly every night, she had to go out on the circles and dance till the moon set. She was cold, too, for in place of her warm frocks she had nothing in the world but Scarlet Mantle's old clothes, made of rose-leaves and gossamer. She might well be hungry also, for the Moths gave her nothing but dew and locusts for food. Still there was one thing more dreadful than all these put together. For some reason or other Lily's tongue had begun to grow very long.

Yes, it was not painful, but exceedingly ugly, as you may imagine. Little by little it increased and grew longer, until she was obliged to tie it round her neck to keep it out of her way, and the Moths were always laughing about it, which made our little girl very melancholy.

The Queen of the Moths was a very motherly person, and Lily soon made friends with her.

"Your Majesty," she said one day, "I am very miserable. Indeed, I think I shall die if I am kept here much longer."

"What is amiss, my child?" inquired the Queen.

"Why am I detained here?" replied Lily. "And why have I so little to eat and drink?"

"My dear child, you know the reason," answered the Queen. "You told a wicked falsehood, and you are paying the penalty for it now."

"Ah! your Majesty, it wouldn't be so bad if I could only get rid of my long tongue," pleaded Lily. "Dear Queen, please can't you rid me of my ugly tongue?"

"No, child, I cannot, but you can rid yourself of it."

"How? Oh, please tell me."

The Queen of the Moths sighed.

"There is only one way," she answered. "Your tongue is disfigured, because it hath offended. If you wish to get rid of it, you must acknowledge your fault and confess the lie you told."

Poor Lily! Like many other children of a larger growth, she was stubborn, and did not like this plan of getting rid of her trouble. Anything rather than saying: "I broke the clock."

So the child went on among the Moths, suffering cold and hunger, midnight dancing, and the big tongue.

But little Lily loved her father and mother, and did not like to be away from them for ever. She began to steal away from the valley, and go to her own home. Often she stood looking in at the window, and saw her father and mother and Teddy sitting with Scarlet Mantle; and the tears would start to her eyes, and run down her cheeks, and she would cry out in her grief, "Oh! I do so wish I was sitting on my own stool again."

One night she was standing by the window particularly unhappy, and in a very penitent mood. Had she but the opportunity, she determined to confess her fault. There sat her father in the full flare of the lamp, thinking he had Lily by his side. There was Teddy with his toys, and while the little outcast was gazing, Jane, the nurse, entered with the tea-tray; cups and saucers began to rattle, and her brother and Scarlet Mantle gathered round the table. Oh, to be shut out from all this comfort, and the smiles and caresses of her parents! At length, something led her father to rise from his seat and look out into the darkness beyond. He opened the window and stepped out upon the verandah. In a moment a tiny hand was thrust into his own, and a timid, hesitating voice was heard to say,—

"I—I am—so—sorry. I—broke—the clock."

"You! Who are you?" cried the father in astonishment.

"I'm Lily, father," she cried out, with a great sob.

"Lily! Why, Lily is in the dining-room with mamma."

"No; *I am* Lily, your own naughty little girl, and—I broke the clock. There!" she sobbed aloud. "The Moths took me away because I told you a falsehood, and they only gave me old faded rose-leaves to wear, and the legs of locusts to eat, and made me drink dew out of the cups of the flowers; and see what a great, long, ugly tongue they have given me for telling that story."

The trilling voice sounded very remorseful, and the little hand clung nervously to the father, who immediately led the little one into the dining-room.

The first thing on which the eyes of the man rested was the vacant seat of Scarlet Mantle.

"Hallo! Where's the other one?" he cried.

"The other one?" repeated his wife. "What other one, dear?"

"The—the child, Lily," replied the astonished pater.

The good woman laughed, and answered, "There she is, at your side."

"Nonsense; this little lady says she has just come from Mothland, and that she is our Lily whom the Moths stole because she told a falsehood over the breaking of the clock. Surely there aren't two Lilys?" and the farmer looked beneath the sofa, under the table, and even up the chimney; but Scarlet Mantle, the moment she saw Lily enter the room, vanished through the window, and of course was not to be found.

"Well, this is a queer go, wife."

"Most extraordinary," responded the mother, gazing with a doubtful look upon the real Lily, who stood quietly looking from one to the other.

"Oh, this is Sis," exclaimed Teddy. "There's the bump on the nose which I made with my ball last week. You're Lily, who smashed the clock, aren't you?" he asked, looking up in her face.

"Indeed, Teddy dear, I'm your little sister, and it was I who broke the clock, and the Moths took me away, and gave me this big, frightful tongue, because I said I didn't. You see here——"

And she put up her hand to her mouth, but lo! the ugly member had vanished. How glad she felt that it was gone! The mere effort to do right had brought its own reward. And as she repeated again, more earnestly, "I broke the clock, and I want you to forgive me," her father saw she was really his own little girl, and giving her a hearty kiss of forgiveness, seated her in her own accustomed place at table, and they were very happy once more.

That night Lily slept soundly in her own room, in her own cosy bed, and she thought it much better than dancing till she was tired round the Moth circles by the river-bank.

And so thought the Scarlet Mantle!

# MOONLAND.

## CHAPTER I.

SOME of our relatives on the other side of the globe will be astonished to learn that the way to the Moon has been discovered by an unfortunate member of the *literati* of Australia.

The greatest thinkers of the day have scouted the idea as nothing but moonshine, when spoken to about the practicability of the discovery. But it must be borne in mind that the same laws of Nature which guide and rule the Mother Country are somewhat erratic here at the Antipodes, inasmuch as we are all *upside down*—standing on our heads, in fact. Therefore we are prepared for marvels. In a land where there are animals who stand on their *tails*, and fight with all four feet at once; where the young leap out of and into their parents' stomachs at will—there being a strange bag in that quarter for the purpose of humouring the antics of the juveniles, just like the hole in the bow of a timber ship; where there are creatures that appear neither flesh nor fowl—who swim in ponds like a duck, have a duck's bill, who lay eggs, yet have feet and hair like a beast; in a land where the leaves on the trees grow edgeways to the sun, and the trees themselves shoot downwards, surely it is no great wonder that we have found a passage to the great luminary of night, and had the pleasure of shaking hands and likewise supping with the disobedient man who gathered sticks on Sunday.

The scientific world will never feel half the surprise anent our new discovery as that which fell upon the old shepherd when he found himself surrounded and made a prisoner. He had left his sheep in charge of the only companion he had in these regions—viz., his dog. Within a sheltered nook on one of the fairest and most luxuriant slopes of the mysterious Blue Mountains, Patch, the half-bred dingo, held watch and ward over his charge while his master wandered down the rugged side of the cliff in search of gold. Here the sun was almost hid behind the broad awning of gigantic trees, whose immense trunks, gnarled and hoary with age, stood like mammoth sentinels to guard the dim glen below. The lonely herdsman had often descended to that spot before unmolested, but now from every mound and hollow there peered the grotesque faces of the Mountain Sprites, watching his every movement, until with a sudden rush they pounced upon him and held

"HE WAS BORNE ALONG SO SWIFTLY THAT HE NEARLY LOST HIS SENSES."

him fast. For a time he struggled manfully to free himself. It was quite useless. The genii of the Blue Mountains are a powerful people, not to be trifled with, as the shepherd soon discovered.

He was lifted bodily up, and borne along so swiftly that he nearly lost his senses. The route of his captors lay in a downward direction—never *upward*. And it appeared as if the dusky ravines which they traversed led right away from the upper world into the region of eternal night.

"Dear friends, good people, where are you taking me?" cried the poor fellow in an affrighted tone.

"Bis, bus, silence, mortal!" replied an ancient gnome authoritatively. "Your destination is not on the Earth, but the Moon."

"Good gracious!" ejaculated the poor shepherd, with starting eyeballs.

"Bus, peace," rejoined the brownie in a whisper. "The voice of man hath never disturbed these solitudes since the creation."

"Gentlemen, pray let me go!"

"Art thou not going, thou dissatisfied mortal? Be silent."

"It is all up with me," groaned the unfortunate captive.

"Nay, verily, it will be all down with thee," answered the sprite. "Behold!"

As the fairy spoke they emerged into a dismal spot, in the midst of which gaped a wide, black pit; at the mouth of the chasm the shepherd beheld the forms of two beings in shape like the fabled vampires, who clapped their tremendous wings in ecstasy at sight of him.

"Who is this?" they cried.

And the fairies answered, "A visitor for Moonland."

"No, no, I'm not going to the Moon," replied the trembling shepherd.

The horrid vampires laughed in exultation at his misery, and the sound shook the walls of the solid cliffs around. "Hear me, Dusk, and thou, Lunar," said the gnome, addressing the winged monsters. "This fellow hath had the impudence to invade our sacred precincts, and attempted to release some of our dreaded foes, the 'Gold Nuggets' whom we have made prisoners. What shall we do with the rascal?"

"Send him to the Moon," they cried with one voice.

"Mercy, gentlemen, mercy."

"Fiddlesticks! To Moonland with him," answered the sprite. "There is lots of room for him to fossick there. Eh, Lunar?"

Over that terrible void, near where they held him, our hero observed a strange object floating with a gentle, oscillating motion, as a feather floats in space. In appearance, it was like a gigantic umbrella inverted, with a hole cut in the centre. To the ends of the ribs cords of gossamer were fastened which stretched upward to a car in the shape of a star, the points expanded like huge wings. The nature of this material, or by what process this curious vehicle had been manufactured, the unfortunate shepherd had neither power nor leisure at that moment to examine, for the ancient fay had no sooner spoken than Dusk and his companion seized hold of him, like a pair of vultures, and flew upward with him in the car of the parachute.

"Good-bye, Lunar, let me know when you arrive," cried some of the fairies.

"Slide a message down a moonbeam," responded others.

"Or a rainbow, or the tail of a comet." And while the mountain sprites stood and jeered, the quaint machine suddenly shot down the empty space with the velocity of a cannon-ball.

Who shall describe the sensation of the poor mortal, as he felt himself falling—falling down—down, a blind mass, through the darkened air? Those who have fallen, or have leaped even from a moderate height, can have no conception of the frenzied terror that took possession of him for a moment. Yet it was only for a moment. Strange to say, he did not lose his presence of mind, and his fear left him as suddenly as it had fallen upon him. From a bewildering chaos of thought in the captive's mind *curiosity* became paramount to all else. Amid the murky blackness around and about there was very little to examine, but the shepherd thrust his head through the gossamer network of the machine and gazed below. Far, far away in the profound depths beneath them, he saw a vast disc of soft light which threw its rays upward, and enabled him to discern that the abyss through which they were descending appeared like a hollow cone, the neck of which began in the mountain, and like an eddying circle in the water, gradually became wider and wider as they advanced.

The progress of the parachute was so swift that they rapidly emerged into the focus of the light—the wide mouth of the cone receding to a faint, dark circle on the pale horizon in the space of a few seconds. It was astounding how wondrous soft and beautiful the shimmering glow of light in this new region burst upon the mortal's vision. He had witnessed many lovely changes from the lofty peaks of the New South Wales Alps, but Dame Nature had never presented herself to his eyes in such a garb before. Not the glaring, hot, dazzling rays of the summer sun here, but rather a gentle, subdued, dreamy refulgence, without the ghost of a shadow or shade of variation upon anything.

Above, below, one universal, pale, liquid glimmer, devoid of vapour. Distant mountains, peaked and gabled like an iceberg, appeared to view, and hills and valleys, with deep ruts and chasms, forming an amphitheatre of vast dimensions, became more clear to the sight every moment. Everything seemed mixed up and confounded by the uniformity of colour. Rocks, valleys, and streams presented a weird and wonderful aspect under new conditions where, like Hoffmann's shadowless man, every object was lighted up on all sides, equally, in the absence of a central point. Scorched and charred and burnt, there was not a sign of a tree or a shrub on the face of the whole landscape. Scoriæ and dross and pumice-stone—nothing else, save the waters that lay bathed in luminous silvery grey.

From the vast panorama our hero turned his eyes upon his companions, the vampires. They had cast the netting of the car aside.

"Prepare thyself, mortal," cried Lunar in a terrible voice.

"Prepare myself, for what?"

"For a header into the sea yonder beneath us," answered the vampire coolly.

"Good heavens! Gentlemen, you really don't think I can dive from this great height! I shall be dashed to mincemeat," responded the shepherd, in a tone of consternation.

The monsters only laughed at him, and repeated their command.

"Descend a little lower, good Lunar. Do, gentle Dusk," he pleaded.

"We can't. This is Moonland. Not enough *gravity* here," they replied.

"Moonland! Mercy on me! And shall I have to leave my old bones in the Moon?" cried he in despair.

"Plenty of 'em here—loads. Valleys full, as you'll find. Come, jump!"

"I won't!" cried the shepherd in a savage tone. Whereupon the monsters caught him with their claws, and threw him headlong from the car.

The fall was frightful to contemplate, and I'm afraid it will be necessary to allow the poor fellow seven days to recover his equilibrium.

## CHAPTER II.

IF the unhappy mortal had been capable of thinking at the moment he was hurled from the car by the vampires, it is more than probable that his mind would have presented the picture of a terrible and instantaneous death. Strange to relate, instead of the rushing, headlong plunge downward, to be anticipated under the conditions, our hero found himself gently floating in space with the buoyancy of one of the feathered tribe. The dread and fear of death were lost, or rather swallowed up in a nameless terror, at the unnatural position in which he was placed. Yet there was no mystery in it. According to a well-known law, the weight of bodies diminishes as they descend from the outside of the Earth. It is at the surface of the globe where weight is most sensibly felt, and it is just possible that, had we accompanied the shepherd through the thick crust of the terrestrial sphere, we should have soon discovered, as he did, that beyond, at the *other side*, there is little or no gravity at all. Hence his peculiar position. Indeed, it was most fortunate that the old man chanced to have several nuggets of gold in his pockets at the time, otherwise, I'm afraid he would have been suspended in mid-air like Mohammed's coffin. As it happened, gold turned the scale, even in Moonland, and enabled the adventurous mortal to descend in a horizontal rather than a vertical course to the shores of the Moon.

Within his vision below lay a vast expanse of water; the rugged coast bordered with majestic hills, torn by earthquakes, and blasted and ravaged by volcanic fires. The waves broke on this shore with a dull, hollow noise against the cliffs. Some of these, dividing the coast with their sharp spurs, formed capes and promontories, fantastic in form and worn by the ceaseless action of the surf. It was like a continuous cosmical phenomenon, filling a basin of sufficient extent to contain an inland sea, and walled by enormous mountains with the irregular shores of Earth, but desert, and fearfully wild.

If the eyes of the shepherd were able to range afar over this sea, it was because the shadowless light brought to view every detail of it. The expanse above him was a sky of huge plains of cloud, pale yellow in colour, and drifting with rapidity athwart the firmament, where appeared dark circles, rings and cones, in lieu of stars. Everything that he could liken to aught on this globe seemed changed by some potent power into opposite extremes. Downward, slowly but surely, without the faculty to change his course either to the right or to the left, the mortal at length plunged into the water. He was a capital swimmer, and had no fear of being drowned. Imagine his dismay, however, when he found himself sinking to the bottom like a crowbar, in spite of his vigorous efforts to keep afloat. In vain he struck out and struggled desperately to rise to the surface by use of legs and arms. Vain and useless. Down he went, plumbing the depths below, until he touched the bottom; then, to his surprise, he rebounded back again like a cork, but only to go down again as speedily as before.

The poor fellow had been pertinaciously holding his breath, as is customary when bathing in terrestrial streams; and therefore when he could no longer resist the unconquerable will of nature to draw breath, judge of the consternation which laid hold of him, when, instead of the choking gasp of suffocation anticipated, he found little difficulty in respiration! In fact, that vast sheet was not water at all, such as he knew it, but a subtle fluid, half way between a liquid and a gas, which, though heavier than air, was yet so much lighter than water that it was impossible for him to float in it.

These discoveries come to him in quick succession, and created within his mind the most un-

"He was not certain whether the monster was leaping or flying."

*Australian Fairy Tales.*] [*Page* 269.

speakable astonishment. By degrees, and after many attempts, he found that he could walk along the bed of this strange sea with comparative ease. Accordingly he straightway reached the shore and sat down on the cliffs to rest. Wonder upon wonder had crowded so fast and thick upon the bewildered mind of our traveller that his thoughts were in a whirl. Yet another surprise was in store for him, for as he extended his vision over the landscape he beheld a gigantic creature approaching with prodigious bounds and flying leaps. In his utter amazement he believed one of the rugged hills had been suddenly endowed with life, and was hurrying on to crush him. Never before had the eyes of breathing mortal rested on such a mammoth of human outline. No, nor upon anything with such power of movement. He was not certain whether the monster was leaping or flying, but he was quite positive as to its extraordinary swiftness.

In his terror the shepherd fled—when lo! he found that *he too* was endowed with this singular force of locomotion. It is surprising how fear lends a man wings. The terrestrial one didn't need anything of the kind, though. Incredible the springs and leaps he made over the high peaks, across chasms and cliffs, and along the steep mountain-sides; wonderful the feeling which changed from dread to exuberant delight and ecstasy, and again to terror, as the mighty voice of the pursuer came upon his ears like a peal of thunder.

"Halt! Stop! Who art thou?"

Had he been then and there endowed with wings, the old shepherd felt that he could not escape from the owner of that voice. All he could do was to cast himself flat on his face and await his doom in silence.

"Shall Greencheese utter his command twice? Who art thou?" repeated the mammoth.

"Mercy, your Highness. I am only old Bob, the shepherd of the Blue Mountains, New South Wales.

"Old Bob! Blue Mountains! Ha! Fuddle-fum. Well?"

"Some fairies got hold of me t'other day, and bundles me down here, on a sort of humberellar, your Worship; that's all I knows about it," cried the mortal in a despairing tone.

"Fairies! Mum! I know the rogues," responded the creature quickly. "Many a summer's night I have watched their freaks and gambols among secluded nooks and dells hidden away from mortal ken. Many a long hour we have held converse together, in the silent ravines and woods, when all the human mites of the Australian world were locked in sleep. Go on!"

"I knows noffin' more, sir, only that I shouldn't like to leave my old body *here*!" cried Bob.

"Ha! Buncham! Fi-pho—fiddle-faddlem! Thou shalt live."

"Thanks, your Highness." And the shepherd lifted his eyes and gazed upon his companion. The Colossus at Rhodes, towering high above the lofty gables of the aged city, was but a pigmy in comparison. Ancient, hoary Sphinx of the Egyptians, standing for countless years on the shores of Father Nile, would have seemed a thing of yesterday beside it. Nay, that primitive marvel, the figure of wood discovered in Joppa, aged five thousand years, could reckon itself an infant in proximity to this lunarian.

Save the round, full, Chinese-like face, with its accompanying tremendous mouth, and the faint outline of the human form, there was nothing further to assist description of the creature except that he was high and bulky beyond conception, and quite as transparent as a lighted lantern. The face wasn't at all unpleasant. It beamed with such a broad, friendly, yet withal humorous, expression as it gazed down upon Bob, that the mortal found courage to address it.

"Please, who be you, sir?"

"Me? I'm the *Man in the Moon*, of course," replied the creature, smiling.

"Eh! Why, dash my old jumper, if I didn't think as I'd seen your countenance before!" answered the old herdsman with animation. "I can tell yer, as ye comes out pretty strong sometimes on them 'ere mountains t'other side of Sydney. Why, I've yarded many a thousand sheep, and you've been a-looking at me all the while, eh?"

The Man in the Moon nodded.

"Ah, and I'll bet you knows my old dog, Patch?"

Another nod in the affirmative.

"Brayvo! old boy. Why, we're old chums. Shake hands."

"We never shake hands in the Moon, Bob; but I'll embrace you," cried the lunarian, smiling; and suiting the action to the word, he suddenly enveloped the mortal in such a broad beam of refulgence that the old fellow appeared as if cased in polished armour.

In accordance with the etiquette of Moonland, it would be rude to disturb their *tête-à-tête* before next Saturday.

## CHAPTER III.

"THE presumptuous beings on earth have the impudence to tell their children that the Moon is made of *green cheese*," quoth the mammoth.

"Indeed, sir, but that is very true," answered Bob. "When I was a boy I believed it was only a big cheese, and I can safely say that when I've seen it in the water, up at Bathurst, where we lived, I've been silly enough to wade into the water arter it, thinking to take it home and have my supper off it."

"Ah, it's rare fun to watch the moon-rakers try to grasp my shadow, Bob."

"I believe you, sir. Lord, how you must laugh in your sleeve at 'em! Your Moonship must look down upon many a strange sight," said the shepherd reflectively.

The Man in the Moon smiled widely. "Humph! I look upon all kindred of the terrestrial world," he answered gravely. "I am but the pale reflection of the great luminary, the Sun, whose slave I am. When he fadeth from the surface of the globe, I borrow his beams and become the watchman of the night. The mighty human beings, and the lowly; rich and poor; the sinful and the good, are all beneath my vision. I watch the murderer crawling with stealthy feet towards his victim, and I note the robber lying in wait to plunder; I haunt the gloom where guilt and misery lie huddled together in rags. Wickedness in high places cannot escape me. Over the deep sleep of toiling millions my beams hold watch and ward, kissing the rosy lips of innocence, where yet lingers the soft breath of prayer. Hovering o'er the sighing maiden and the restless miser, weaving fancies which fill the poet's brain with unutterable poesy, and with such shapes as live only in dreams of age and infancy, and vanish with the light of morn. Cuddlephum! Bobberish—Baa-lamb! Bo!"

"Just so," said Bob, opening wide his eyes at the strange words. "I begs to say that French wasn't taught at the school I went to. Howsoever, I'm quite willing to dine with you, if that's what you mean. I'm beginning to feel pereshious hungry, I can tell yer."

"Hungry! Base mortal, there is no such word known here," echoed the monster.

"Good heavens! No eating!" cried Bob, aghast.

"None."

"Scissors! I'm afraid visitors from Australia won't overrun Moonland, if that's the case."

"Peace! Follow me, and thou shalt taste nectar,

which shall banish the cravings of thy vulgar race."

The Man in the Moon bounded away over the pumice-stone crags like a gigantic kangaroo, followed by Bob. Chaos and desolation were everywhere visible around them. Sad indeed and supremely melancholy looked the place. Mountains riven asunder; vast ravines and valleys choked with bleached bones of monsters unknown to men; immense plains, scattered thickly with the fossil remnants of ages; mingled dust and huge mounds of bony fragments of animal and reptile, which a thousand Cuviers could never have reconstructed. Up the rugged zigzags with tremendous leaps, echoless, shadowless, and across the dust, silent to their footfall, went the lunarian and the mortal.

"This is a dreary place, sir," muttered the latter, almost breathless in his haste.

"Peace, or perchance the forms of these dead monsters will rise to rebuke thee!" answered his companion solemnly. "Here, where thou art standing, these enormous animals of the first period lived and roved at will. The human mind cannot conceive their colossal proportions, for they were extinct many ages before the advent of man."

The shepherd followed his conductor in silence, wondering if it were possible that these mighty dead could take shape again and swallow him at one snap. Jonah had been bolted by a whale, but the skeletons of these creatures appeared large enough to engulf a hundred whales a day, and twice that number of Jonahs into the bargain.

Bob was almost ready to sink down amid the Golgotha when the Man in the Moon halted before a very high mountain. Making a sign to his companion to follow, he quickly disappeared from view. At first it seemed as if the mammoth had vanished within the mountain, but the mortal saw an opening at the base which he entered. What a study for a geologist! In the dim ages of the past, when the satellite of our Earth seethed and boiled as a vast crater, the solid intestines of this cone, yielding to some great power below it, had been riven in twain, leaving an unmeasurable grotto of winding galleries. Toiling along in the wake of the lunarian, the captive trod on a broad aisle, on each side of which rose a series of arches succeeding each other, like the noble arcades of some Gothic cathedral. Obelisk-like massive pillars stood out from the rent wall like mighty sentinels guarding the wreck. Had our hero been a mineralogist, armed with his hammer, his steel pointer, his magnetic needles, and his blow pipe, what a fund of information he might have gleaned here to place before the spectacles of professors and philosophers! Nay, had he but possessed the faintest idea of the science of building, what patterns, what studies around and above him, for every form of the art to hereafter confound architects of the nineteenth century!

Poor Bob was neither a mineralogist nor an architect, so he passed by these things without a second glance, and entered a vaulted chamber, upon whose round, jagged dome rested the whole weight of the mountain; the dented projections and the sharp points on wall and roof spun into an endless network of lines and seams, luminous as all things here seemed to be, and changing colour from silver-grey to deep crimson.

Wonder had lost its functions for Bob the shepherd, otherwise he would have stood aghast at the strange forms moving to and fro within this chamber; round in shape, and taller than giants of long ago, with arms and legs evidently telescoped at the joints, so that they could lengthen or shorten them at will, and each shedding their quota of refulgence to illuminate the scene. Monster glow-worms, gigantic fire-flies, with the trickery of monkeys, and the strength of bears, seized the shrinking man, and rose with him to the dome, which opened instantly and engulfed them. Amidst a circle of light, which changed quicker than the sparkles of a diamond, the poor shepherd found he was being borne upward and hemmed in by a ring of these natives of the Moon—upward and yet upward, without will to pause or stop, the mad whirlwind of light ever changing, red, blue, grey, yellow, white, azure, and the legion gathering in increased numbers every moment round him until the climax came, and the crater, that had been silent for countless ages, once more opened its ponderous jaws, casting him forth as a rocket, where—amidst fiery rings and bars, and blazing stars of light—he fell down, down, down into darkness and oblivion!

\* \* \* \* \*

"I say, mate, how far is it to the Blue Mountains Inn?"

Old Bob, the shepherd, rubbed his eyes and looked up at the questioner. He was a stout, thick-set fellow, with a heavy swag on his back, and a black billy-can in his hand.

The man had to repeat his query ere the herdsman found speech.

"Why, surely, *you're* not the Man in the Moon, eh?" asked Bob, with a wild stare.

The swagman stepped backward a pace or two, and regarded our hero with more attention.

"Man in the Moon!" he repeated. "Why, the old fellow's gone off his head."

"'WHY, SURELY, *YOU'RE* NOT THE MAN IN THE MOON?'"

"Where's the others with the long legs and arms?" and the shepherd shuddered.

"He's cranky, sure enough," muttered the traveller audibly. "The coves as you were asking arter are all gone," he said aloud. "You get up on your pins, or they'll be back again

Here's a bob; come now, hook it, or they'll have you," saying which the swagman went on his way.

Our hero raised himself into a sitting posture. Before him lay the verdant slopes and ridges of the mountain, bathed in sunlight. Yonder his sheep fed peacefully, watched by the faithful Patch. Then the old man raised his vision higher than the earth and thanked Heaven that he was still safe and sound on *terra firma*.

# "SAILOR."

THAT great painter of animals, Sir Edwin Landseer, never sketched a nobler specimen of the canine race than the big, black, curly Newfoundland dog, Sailor, the hero of our story. He was a fine, faithful dog, and almost as large as a young foal, and every bit as frisky and as harmless, save when teased by naughty boys. If you tried ever so hard you couldn't hide anything from Sailor. You might fasten him in a room and then attempt to conceal a ball, or a piece of wood, in the garden or the stables, but the moment you set him free Sailor would hunt the object out and return with it in his mouth. Besides being sagacious, the faithful brute could dive and swim like a fish; that is why he received such a suitable name.

Captain Hauser, of the barque *South Australian*, had brought him from India when but a puppy, but now the worthy captain had settled down ashore with his two boys at Anchordale on the

River Murray, and the dog had become almost one of the family circle.

On a very hot afternoon, and when the New Year was scarcely a score of days old, Bertie Hauser and his cousin, Tom Blake, took it into their heads to have a row down the river. Anchordale was a pleasant cottage situated on the bank of the Murray, with a tiny skiff fastened to a stout post at the end of the orchard.

Bertie was only eight years of age, and Tom one year older; but the boat being so small and light they managed to get afloat and paddled away in high glee down the river. The dog, Sailor, was the only one who had seen them depart, and he, with wagging tail and out-hanging tongue, had begged, as only dumb animals can, to accompany them on their trip; but Tom Blake said the boat would be swamped with such a cargo, and so the lads had departed without him. Now, although Sailor was dumb, he wasn't blind. Neither was the poor brute wanting in instinct. Many a day he had acted as a substitute for a pony for little Bertie, and had even suffered the child to put a string into his mouth for a bridle, and had trotted or cantered and walked up and down the lawn according to the whim of his infantile rider. Indeed, Sailor was a kind old dog, and probably thought it his duty to guard the person of his young master, on land or on the water.

Perhaps this instinct prompted the Newfoundland to crawl cat-like through the dense scrub on the bank of the river and keep the skiff in view. Be that as it may, the dog never lost sight of them for a moment. He saw Tom Blake guide the boat into a wide part of the stream, and where the banks were very high and almost as steep as the gable of a house.

"Oh, Bertie, here's the place for a bathe. Are you game?" asked Tom, rocking the boat.

Bertie assented. They found a little cove, where they landed, and made fast the skiff; then ascending the high bank they began to prepare for the water. Both boys had been taught to swim —as all boys should be—but Bertie and his cousin had been warned not to bathe down the river, because there were places teeming with snags and dangerous undercurrents. Tom and his companion had forgotten all about the caution. The water at this spot appears very dark and still and cool, with the shadows of the overhanging trees upon it, and the drooping branches of the willows laving to and fro on its bosom with a dreamy sound.

"What a frightful jump!" cried Bertie, approaching the brink timidly, and looking over at the river beneath. "It's a high leap, Tom; hadn't we better go a little farther down?"

"Not at all," responds Tom, swinging his arms about above his head. "I like a good header; you stand there and watch me dive."

Bertie stands aside and watches him. Tom retires several paces, starts forward with a short, quick run, and springs headforemost from the cliff into the river. For a moment the waters bubble and widen out in circling eddies over the broad expanse. Bertie Hauser stands looking down trying to trace the white, shapely form of his cousin cleaving through the dark stream, expecting to see him rise to the surface twenty yards away from where he plunged in. But many seconds go by, and Tom Blake rises not, and poor Bertie, in an agony of suspense, calls to him to "come up at once, or he will be drownded," as if the treacherous element would part its substance and carry his weak voice below, to its holes and caves, where his companion is struggling for his little life.

"Tom, Tom, dear cousin Tom," cries the child on the bank, as the truth begins to dawn upon him that Tom is drowning. "Oh! what shall I do to help him? What shall I do?" When lo! old

Sailor comes bounding towards him with a joyous bark. The boy clutches his favourite by the ears and draws him forward to the brink of the river, where, pointing down to the water, he urges on the dog with voice and gesture. "Ho, Sailor, fetch him out, old fellow, go on—bring him out."

Sailor needs no second bidding. Before Bertie has the words out of his mouth, the dog comprehends the whole business, and leaps into the water and disappears. How anxiously the child watches for his re-appearance! At a spot half way up the stream, he observes the water begin to whirl and eddy and bubble upward, as being disturbed by a great commotion beneath; and here Sailor rises to the surface, and blows the water from his snout, like a whale; but the dog is alone. There is no sign of poor Tom Blake. Little Bertie becomes sick and faint with terror, but the boy does not lose his presence of mind. He has every confidence in the Newfoundland's strength and courage.

"Ho, Sailor, fetch him out, old boy, bring him out."

Downward plunges the gallant dog again, while his young master, naked as he is, rushes down to the skiff, jumps in, and pushes into midstream, running athwart the dog, as he rises once more.

This time Sailor has something in his mouth, but the boat knocking against him causes him to let go. Yet he dives after it, and appears again in a moment with the drowning boy. Sailor has clutched him firmly by the hair of the head, and the dog's great red eyes are all aflame as he buoys up the insensible child and paddles the water with ponderous strokes and lands him safe upon the bank.

What avail little Bertie's terms of endearment and the affectionate appeals he makes to his still, silent cousin? Tom Blake is deaf. And although Bertie may make a hundred promises of bats and guns and ponies poor Tom cannot hear him.

It is fortunate that two men with swags upon their backs are passing at the time, who carry the unfortunate youth into the sunlight, and rub his body vigorously with their hands until the vitality that was almost extinct begins to revive again within him.

When Tom had partly recovered and could speak, he told his uncle, the captain, that when he dived he struck his head against a snag, which rendered him insensible, and no doubt in that state he was being carried away by the current when the dog found him.

And poor Tom was grateful for the service, for

when he was quite well he bought the Newfoundland a grand collar, and had the following inscription engraven on it:—

"SAILOR,
"Rescued *Tom Anson Blake* from drowning on the 18th January, 187—, at Anchordale, River Murray."

# NELLIE.

## CHAPTER I.

RAIN, rain—nothing but rain on this Christmas Eve, in the New South Wales metropolis. Although it was in the heat of summer the wind from the coast blew keenly through the almost deserted streets, and caused the fine mist-like wet to penetrate the stoutest overcoat. It was such weather that no one who had a roof over his head would care to be out in. But there was one wearily toiling from street to street, beneath the protection of the verandahs—a delicate-looking girl. With one hand she was trying to wrap her scanty rags round her wasted body, and in the other she held a half-dozen boxes of wax matches. Her face was worn, and pinched, and dirty, but it was a very beautiful, patient, little face; her hair, too, would have been a bright golden in natural hue, save that it was shaggy and dirty also. It was to little purpose that she offered her matches to the passers-by, who were few and far between on this wet evening—they were all too anxious to get home out of the rain. From the brightly lighted streets the little wanderer crossed Hyde Park, and wended her way slowly up Oxford Street, and from thence to the left, along the Bay Road, where dwell the wealthy and the great. Why she had left the shops and all the busy part of the city for the wide, bleak road, dotted with high, massive houses standing out dark and cold in the falling rain, the poor child could not tell. Impelled by some strange fascination, she had quitted her usual haunts, and taken the opposite direction leading from her wretched home. Although it was getting late, and past the time when she should have returned, she had no thought of going home. Her memory was full of faint, indistinct thoughts, whether dreams or far-away realities, who shall say? She wondered why she had rambled so far from the city; but she also felt she must go on. Her ragged dress was soaked with rain and the keen wind was cruel and cutting, yet the poor little thing did not feel the rain or the wind; on the contrary, she felt as if she was on fire, save now and then there would pass a cold feeling all over her, which caused a shivering fit. The match girl was well aware that she would be beaten when she returned to her wretched dwelling, yet, strange to say, she felt perfectly happy as she wandered farther away from it.

Half way up the Bay Road there came over the little waif a feeling of dizziness, accompanied by a feeling of thirst, and again that burning sensation which again changed into a cold shiver, as she stood there. Close at hand there was a friendly porch belonging to a grand mansion, so the child crept into it, out of the wind and rain, and crouched down. No sooner had she done so than all her light-heartedness appeared to leave her, and she burst into tears. It was very strange that directly the little match vendor began to cry she heard a confusion of sounds around her—wild, mocking laughter, and shouts, and stamping of feet, and strange lights were dancing before her eyes. The stones on which she was lying seemed to be heaving and tossing, and she felt very frightened just for a moment, and then she fell fast asleep.

These sounds still went on in her slumber, but they gradually got softer and softer, and sweeter and more subdued, until they changed into the most lovely music. And the little outcast thought she was standing in the midst of a very beautiful garden, and somehow it appeared to her that she had known it all a long time ago. The rain and wind and the murky clouds had passed away, and it was glorious, sunny day; the flowers were in full bloom. Voices of birds and insects filled the balmy air, and gay coloured butterflies flitted here and there. While she was standing, wondering that all these strange things should seem so familiar to her, a handsome boy, with golden curls, approached, and exclaimed,—

"Oh, dear sister Nellie, come and play. Why did you go away and stay away so long?"

The dreamer looked up; she appeared to know the happy face quite well, and she assured him in a voice, that was not like her old thin, weak voice, but soft and clear, which seemed like a voice that had belonged to her a long, long time ago,—

"Indeed, I don't know where I have been, Frank; nor why I went away. Is it a long time since?" she asked timidly.

"Such a long time, sister."

"I am here at last, Frank; and I will never go away again. Come, let us play in the garden." And then she took his hand, and they walked on together amongst the flowers, while the thousand voices round about gave gladsome welcome. All the old miserable life of the beggar child seemed to fade quickly away here, leaving nothing save the feeling that she had always been accustomed to the grand objects by which she found herself surrounded.

"Suppose we have a game of hide and seek?" suggested Frank.

"That will be very nice; but who shall hide first?"

They had a little consultation about that very important matter, when it was decided that Nellie should hide first. It was most peculiar that the name *Nellie* came quite natural to the dreamer, though she had been called Maggie, Meg, and sometimes Peggy as long as she could remember.

So Nellie went to hide, and she hid behind a rosebush, and there she found a great hole in the ground big enough for her to creep into. Ere she had settled herself, Nellie found that the hole led to a dark passage, with a soft light glimmering at the end of it. Still wondering, she went towards the light. Passing along through several archways, the child emerged into a splendid cavern, lit up with many coloured, sparkling lights from thousands of precious stones, with which the sides and roof of the place were studded. While she was standing awe-struck with amazement at this magnificent place, she heard by her side a flutter of light wings, and turning, saw hovering

NELLIE. 233

over her a beautiful little creature with long hair, which glittered like woven sunbeams. The form was rose-hued in colour, and from its shoulders sprang green wings, sheeny and lustrous as the throat of a humming-bird.

"THE LOVELY BEING TOOK NELLIE BY THE HAND."

"Come!" warbled the being, and the voice was dreamy and sweet, like the "coo" of a stock dove. "Come, and I will show you something wonderful."

And the lovely being took Nellie by the hand, and led the child through a cleft in the rock to another room which was lined, roof, walls, and floor, with soft green moss. All round the room were hung beautiful garlands adorned with diamonds. Some fairly blazed again with gems, others contained only a few, fixed here and there, while fairy-like forms flitted to and fro continually, bearing in their hands more gems, which they fixed into the garlands. The dreamer was very much surprised at what she beheld.

"Where do they get all those diamonds to put into the garlands?" she inquired of her companion.

"The diamonds," answered her conductor, "are the tears of sorrow shed by the unhappy people in the world; for always while they are weeping there are unseen watchers ready waiting to receive their tears and convey them here."

"And what are those very large gems, that shine so brightly in the middle of the finished garlands?"

"Those are tears of joy; no garland can be finished without *them*."

The child wandered round the chamber, and saw that almost all the wreaths had some tears of joy and some of sorrow; but she came at last to one that was quite full of tears of sorrow and in it no tears of joy at all, while on it was a name, "*Peggy the Beggar.*"

Scarcely had her eyes fallen upon the name than she awoke; awoke, and beheld bending over her a lady with a lovely face; but she looked proud and stern, and the little wanderer instinctively shrank away from her and crouched closer to the wall.

"How very tiresome that this wretched child should choose my porch, of all places, to creep into for shelter," cried the lady, in a cold, unfeeling tone. "Yet I cannot turn the unfortunate thing away on such a night as this. It's a poor Christmas indeed for the poor child," she added, in a more tender way. "Here, Smith, take up this little beggar and carry her to the kitchen, give her something to eat, and tell Jane to put some dry things on her."

A tall servant came forward and lifted the ragged bundle of humanity in his arms as tenderly as a mother would have done. The man had just such another little girl at home, and his heart yearned with sympathy for the outcast as he bore her along the great hall of the house. Certainly the place was strange to the child; but as in her dream she seemed to remember everything, so now it appeared to her that the objects upon which she gazed had been familiar to her a long, long time ago, and her dream came back to her so vividly that she cried out aloud, "Oh, Frank! Frank! Dear brother, where are you hiding? Do come to me. Come to sister Nellie. I am not playing now."

The stern lady had followed her servant with his living burden; but when that cry reached her she stopped short, and grasped at the wall for support. What sudden spasm caused the beautiful, haughty face to grow instantly pale, and the tall form to bend trembling down as if struck with palsy?

"Oh, Frank, come to sister Nellie. Dear brother, come."

With a wild, hysterical sob the stately figure bowed lower yet, and pressed her arms upon her throbbing bosom as if each of the little outcast's words had been cruel dagger-thrusts that were piercing her through and through.

Coldness, pride, the vigorous will, that moulds martyrs and devils alike, was strong within the woman, yet the combination of all three had no power against that weak out-cry—"Come to sister Nellie, Frank!"

Ere the low, faint wail had died out, the proud lady had snatched the poor child to her bosom, and covering the hot, unwashed face with passionate kisses, cried aloud,—

"I—I had a darling Nellie once, and a golden-haired boy also, whom we called Frank, but they were buds that faded here to bloom in heaven. And now their dear voices will never fall upon my ears again. Alas! Alas!"

Then like all else she had seen in this place, it seemed to the child that the face of the beautiful lady was not altogether strange to her. The very caress was like the endearing embrace of a mother, whose heart had longed and yearned for her lost ones, and the poor little outcast wondered how it all could be, until she lost all consciousness and began to dream again.

## CHAPTER II.

It was a long and troubled dream. Days and weeks appeared to pass away in which the little sleeper could remember nothing clearly. At one time the beautiful lady would appear to be bending fondly over her, and then the face would change suddenly to that of a wretched hag, whom she had known and called mother, in the miserable home she had within the slums of the city. From this place came terrible voices in her ears, and terrible things struggling round the bed. Flames of fire darted and danced in her poor, weary eyes; but through all this she beheld the fairy of the cavern appear again, holding in his hand the wreath whereon was written her name. He held it towards her gleaming with diamond tear-drops. How she struggled to reach it! The more she tried the weaker she became, but it seemed to her that there was an invisible arm round her for her to rest upon, and though faint and weary, her failing footsteps ever got nearer and nearer the precious circlet. Then followed an interval of soft, soothing quiet, and the eyes of our heroine opened drowsily upon the waking world again. She felt very weak, but somehow very happy. She was lying on a clean, white bed in a comfortable room, which appeared as if she had seen it before somewhere in her dreams. As the child raised her weary eyelids her gaze rested upon the prostrate form of the lady kneeling by her bedside, with her face hidden in the bedclothes, sobbing. The poor wanderer felt sorry that one who had been so kind to her should weep in trouble, and raising her little warm hand, she laid it on the beautiful head of the kneeler, and uttered the familiar word, " Mamma."

The little sufferer knew not why that tender word rose to her lips before any other; she only knew that the affectionate term was in her heart and mind—that was all.

At the sound the grand lady raised her head, and kissed the child again and again with maternal fondness, her lips murmuring the while, "My own darling child. My Nellie, whom I thought had departed from me for ever. Heaven has been good to me."

Then for the first time the little match vendor shed tears of joy. Sleep came to her again, from which she was aroused by the sound of voices talking in whispers close to the bed.

"I am so sorry to have disobeyed you, ma'am, but you must forgive me, and let me stay and nurse my own little pet," cried a girl's voice in pleading accents. "When they told me at home that the stolen child had come home again to you, I couldn't keep away. I know it's all along of my carelessness that she was took away. Yet I loved the deary and was compelled to come, although you must hate the very sight of me."

"Hush, nurse, hush!" replied the lady's voice sadly. "I am so glad you have come. Since I lost my Nellie, and Frank died, and my dear husband perished at sea, I have been a friendless, lonely, and unhappy woman. Now my lost darling has been restored to me again the world will not seem so bleak and weary. You shall stay and help me nurse my stolen baby into health again."

It seemed very strange to the child, as she lay back in the bed, to learn the early history of her own life; how she had been stolen away when she was only a wee toddler; how her brother, just one year older than herself, had pined and died for his sister; how the poor mother, with all her grand and fashionable friends, had felt herself deserted, and had hardened her heart against all good influences, until the cry of the frightened little outcast had reached and softened it.

There were long, weary watchings by the couch of the sufferer, filled with anxiety and suspense. For the mother who had found her lost one had a vague dread haunting her that her darling might be snatched ruthlessly from her a second time, and by a foe more terrible than a kidnapper. The child's sleep was filled with dreams of angels. They carried her again and again to that rocky chamber where hung the garlands; and each time she found her own all ablaze with tears of joy, and nearly finished.

On one occasion she stretched forth her hand to take it, but the fairy came up to her and said,—

"Not yet, my dear; you shall wear it very soon."

The child related these dreams to her mother, who answered nothing, but fell down upon her knees and prayed that the garland should not be completed yet awhile.

Nellie could not understand all this, but one night she felt very weak and cold. Her mother was seated by the bedside gazing with greedy eyes at the poor, worn, pinched-up little face. There were others in the room, but the patient now saw only her mother.

"Dear mamma!"

"What is it, my darling?"

"I have seen the garlands again. Mine is finished at last."

The face of the lady grew very pale. She hid her weeping eyes and muttered,—

"A little while longer, only a little while."

"I know what the garland means *now*, mamma; I am going to die."

"Oh no! my dear, long lost pet, not yet, not yet. I cannot spare you, now you have come back to me. Stay with me a little while—just a little while. You are so very dear to me."

Who shall say what agony of supplication in that low wail of entreaty? Who shall fathom its intensity?

"But you will come too, mamma?" said the weak voice, now grown very weak and feeble. "You have cried so much, your garland must be nearly ready."

A great sob, which shook the tall, shapely figure like a reed, was the only answer. She raised her head at length, and the eyes of mother and child met.

"Oh, when I get there, I'll prepare your garland, mamma," came the faint voice, almost in a whisper now.

For a moment there was a wild light in the poor mother's eyes. The words appeared to stir some old memory in her heart. She looked into the peaceful face of her dying child, and the voice became more calm and steady.

"It is very hard to part, my darling, very hard; but I will try to bear it all, so that tears of joy may mingle with tears of sorrow in my wreath of immortality."

The words fell on an ear that heard them not. There was a look on the child's face that caused the mother to rush forward and throw her arms about the poor weak clay, as if to stay the departing spirit in its flight.

"Oh, mamma! there is little brother Frank with my garland. See! he is beckoning to me."

And then the weary little head fell forward on the mother's shoulder, and the tired spirit entered into rest.

# IN THE CLOUDS.

THEY came to the boy one night when he was abed, and said they would take him with them in their fairy balloon.

Willie Fenton told his father and mother that he had seen the elfins, and what they had promised him, but they only laughed at him and told him he had been dreaming.

Our hero wasn't to be convinced that it was only a dream. Hadn't he seen them—three fairy creatures no higher than his top—enter his bedroom through the keyhole, and seat themselves on his pillow, and begin talking about the glorious sights to be seen in the clouds?

If Willie Fenton had been born up in a balloon his youthful fancy could not have been imbued with a greater passion for the sport. Indeed, since he was a child of four or five years old our youthful aeronaut had blown soap bubbles, and had watched them soar away in the sun, glistening with all the hues of the rainbow, and his dreams at night and aspirations by day had been to emulate those daring spirits who surpassed the mighty eagle in his flight into the bright blue sky above the clouds.

Willie's home, situated on Mount Pleasant, was in the vicinity of many a romantic spot calculated to favour the elves in their adventure, and one fine morning, as the lad was returning from a neighbouring farm, he espied his three nocturnal visitors seated under a large gum-tree awaiting him. Willie recognised them in a moment, and doffing his cap said, " Good-morning, gentlemen."

The fairies rose and saluted him, and answered that they were quite ready to fulfil their promises. Our hero thanked them for their kindness, and at the same time expressed himself quite ready to accompany them. Whereupon the three elves conducted him in silence along a narrow ravine which opened out on a still, quiet glen on the banks of the river. Fastened securely between two huge trees, Willie beheld a great, pear-shaped thing, swaying to and fro with the motion of the breeze, and at which the elves pointed and said, " Behold, our cloud car."

Yes, it was a grand balloon, already inflated and with a cage attached, bordered with wild roses and creepers, that reached from the apex of the monster down to the car beneath, which hung suspended, like a flower-pot in a balcony. How it surged and struggled desperately with the wind, as if it were endowed with life, and wished to escape from fastenings that held it, and soar

"IT WAS A GRAND BALLOON."

upward! And how frail it appeared, as Willie approached and examined it! Was it made of cloth? No, too fine for cloth. Cotton? Nay, it was too soft for cotton, or silk either. Yet the whole fabric seemed no weightier than a gossamer. The fairies smiled at the boy's curiosity, and invited him to enter the car. Our little hero had no sooner complied than the elfins seated themselves at his side. And one of them, who had a bright diadem glittering upon his breast, stood up and waved his hand as a signal, when instantly the balloon shot aloft with inconceivable velocity.

The young mortal closed his eyes and held his breath for one brief moment; but when he looked forth, the earth appeared to be miraculously vanishing from his sight. Although the ascent was fearfully rapid, the motion of the balloon was quite imperceptible. The morning was bright and sunny, the sky a deep, Prussian blue, and as the boy craned his neck over the cage and gazed below, what a glorious sight met his view. There stretched beneath him were the golden valleys of his birthplace, with hundreds of farms dotting the landscape, and no bigger than a child's toy. From his elevated position the houses were as so many dots, and the people in the fields as tiny ants. The flowing Torrens, that had seemed so broad and deep, appeared as a silver thread, and the high cliffs and hills were on a level with the dull round earth. Willie Fenton felt not the least alarm; on the contrary, his courage rose with the balloon, as it sped upward to the sky. The elfin with the diadem threw out some pieces of paper, which seemed to drop like stones. This, however, was not so, but only the effect of the terrible rate at which they were travelling. Higher, higher, still higher. Now they disappeared from view, in a thick vapour forming the white clouds, which looked so light and fleecy from earth. The balloon did not remain long in these, but quickly rose into a clear atmosphere beyond. And here the scene changed to one splendid in the extreme. Above them nothing but the big round sun, and the deep azure of the heavens. Beneath no dingy earth, dim and gloomy, but a brilliant sea of sparkling cloud, rose tinted, dancing and flashing in the sun's rays. The cloud completely hid everything below, and lay beneath like a huge, rolling billow, the top of which flashed back the sunlight till our hero almost fancied it was a wave of driven snow spangled with diamonds. How long Willie might have remained in his rapt trance of wonder it is hard to say, but he was aroused by a feeling of cold, and a difficulty in breathing.

"Our mortal friend will find it very chilly up here," said Pippin, who wore the diadem, answering the boy's unspoken words.

"It has grown very cold indeed, gentlemen," rejoined Willie, his teeth chattering as he spoke.

"Ha, ha! Listen to him, Needle; hear him,

Bobbin; he's beginning to cry out already!" cried Pippin to his companions. "Cold, eh? Well, we have a cure for cold, and for frost and snow—whole mountains of it. Eh, Needle?" As Pippin spoke, he unrolled a parcel which had been lying unnoticed at the bottom of the car, and produced a cloak made of the same material as the balloon. Without more ado they enveloped Willie from head to heel in the garment, with just sufficient space left clear about his eyes so that he could see, the rest of him being completely covered. In a few moments he began to breathe more freely, and the rarity of the air made no impression upon him at all.

"You feel all right now, Willie Fenton?" questioned Bobbin. Willie mumbled, and nodded his head in the affirmative.

"Let us mount higher then, my brethren. Excelsior!" exclaimed Pippin of the diadem. "Bold indeed the mortal who first conceived and carried out the idea of making the unstable element water subservient to his genius, as witness the ships that come and go on the bosom of the ocean; but it is left to us, the elves of Australia, to curb the air and make it do our bidding. Higher and higher go we, to show this mortal the wonders of the upper world."

Upward still, beyond the cloud which breaks

for a moment and gives them a glimpse of the sea, and the coast-line away to the westward seeming no broader than a single thread. And now the cold became intense, but the fairies and their companion felt it not, for their gaze was fixed upon a sight that no emperor or king had ever seen—and perchance never would. If all the diamonds in that rich valley visited by Sinbad the Sailor, also all the gems which Aladdin's lamp could have procured, and all that ever have been seen in the world had been pressed into the service—they would have failed utterly in producing one tithe of the strange sight Willie now saw. The whole dome of the balloon was covered as it were in a diamond mantle. A shower of glittering gems was falling in all directions, apparently coming from the blue void above, and sprinkling down, with a fluttering motion like that of butterflies, and then disappearing in the vast abyss below.

Lost in amazement at this marvellous vision, the boy frees one of his hands, and reaches to catch one of the heavenly gems; but he discovers the diamond shower is in reality only thin sheets of newly-formed ice.

The elves laugh at him and the look of wonder on his face. And Pippin explains in a grave tone, "Boy, we have entered a region where some watery vapour hath been, which the cold hath turned into ice, and now being heavier than the atmosphere falls fluttering to the earth. Towards the earth, I say, since I know well it will never reach it, because before it can do so it will encounter a warmer region, when the ice will again become water and the water vapour. Do you understand?"

"Oh yes. It's the vapour which makes the clouds, isn't it?" answered Willie.

"Just so," replied the elfin. "And now having fulfilled our promise, we will descend again to old mother earth."

Like a streak of light the fairy balloon shot downward through the glittering, diamond shower, through the mist and cloud, until the bright landscape appeared in view. The elfins, Pippin, Needle, and Bobbin, landed Willie safely by the river-bank, and the boy reached home just in time for dinner.

\* \* \* \* \*

The three elves still haunt that dell by the Torrens, so if any of my readers are anxious for a trip in the fairy balloon, I have no doubt Messrs. Pippin & Co. will be only too glad to oblige them—that is, if they are at home.

# WONDERLAND.

MOUNT with me, my little friends, upon the wings of fancy. Don't be alarmed—the conveyance is perfectly safe, and warranted free from accidents. Hi, Presto! Here we stand upon the famous Blue Mountains of our neighbour, whose glens, dells, and deep ravines are haunted by creatures beautiful beyond conception, and grotesque, and stranger than any painter dreamed of. Yonder, on the mountain-side, the western train is seen puffing its way along the gigantic "zigzag," like a huge serpent, and whose hot breath takes weird shapes before it is lost in the blue haze above it. Beneath, on that natural terrace of rock, stands the humble hut of the charcoal-burner, whose single window overlooks a deep valley of monster trees—fallen and half-buried amongst great blocks of stone and rank vegetation.

But who is that woman who is wringing her hands, and calling and weeping by turns, as she runs to and fro among the chaos of undergrowth and the ledges around? It is the wife of the charcoal-burner, and she calls for her two children, who have wandered away and become lost in this wild region. It was early morn when they strolled forth to play—Edith and Winnie, both little toddlers, and quite helpless—yet the sun is on the rim of the horizon and they cannot be found.

"Coo-ee, coo-ee!—Winnie—Edie, my darlings, where are you? Oh, where are you?" cries the poor mother; and her voice grows faint and weary as she calls to the echoing cliffs about. She becomes aware that some one is answering her as she is about to retrace her steps to the hut. The voice is far off at first, but it becomes gradually nearer and nearer, until a rough mountain goat with long horns presents itself before her.

"I am here. What do you want with me?" it said, bowing itself before her.

It was a beautiful animal, with a soft, white, silky fleece, and large, kind-looking eyes, while its voice sounded so full of sympathy that the suffering mother answered readily,—

"Oh, sir! I have lost my two children; pray tell me, have you seen them?"

"I have seen them," answered the goat. "And if you have sufficient courage to follow my advice they shall soon be restored to you. I am the guardian sprite of this glen, which my race have occupied since the Flood. Here on this mountain are two kingdoms; the one on the surface called *Love*; the other, beneath the surface, termed *Hate*. We are ever at war with each other; therefore, I am here to serve you. Learn, O mortal, that Croak and Gloom, of the lower world, have stolen your children, and they have hid them within the bowels of the mountains."

"Then they are dead, and I shall never see them more," replied the woman, falling on her knees and weeping bitterly.

"I have said they shall be restored to you again," replied the goat quickly. "My power is far mightier than the whole nation of Hate combined. Have you faith that I can help you?"

"Yes," she answered, "because *Love* is stronger than *Hate*."

"Good. Extend your hand and pluck a tuft of hair from my right side, roll it in your fingers, then twist it round your finger above your wedding-ring."

The charcoal-burner's wife did as the goat desired her, but she had scarcely finished before the animal vanished from her sight, and she felt herself bodily lifted up, and borne away over the deep ravine, and across over-hanging cliffs and the tops of tall trees, and away down into a yawning chasm, which seemed like a deep and bottomless well. Down, down, she went swiftly, yet with an easy, sliding motion that was not at all unpleasant, while she felt no fear, save for the fate of her little ones. She had a feeling of a powerful presence being near and about her—extending from the finger on which was twisted the goat's hair round and round her person, and beneath her feet, like the strong net-work of a balloon. Even when the void grew dim and black, a strange glow, emanating from the ring, lit up the darkness and revealed to her wondering eyes many earth-bound treasures. Here gleamed thick seams of coal, and there slabs of tin and copper ores, and beyond these shone white masses of stone, like marble, with thick veins of gold therein, which sparkled athwart the woman's eyes, and made her almost forget her children, so great became her desire to possess some of it. While she cogitated she suddenly became conscious that she was upon her feet, standing before a large cavern gate, guarded by a tall griffin, who cried out the moment he espied her, "Who dare enter into the realm of Hate?"

And the woman answered quickly, " Love. Love

dares everything, because, being pure, it is fearless. I have come to demand my children."

The monster laughed at her, and advanced with a large stone to dash out her brains; but the white goat, transformed now into a handsome youth,

"THE MONSTER . . . ADVANCED WITH A LARGE STONE."

with a sharp, gleaming sword in his hand, advanced boldly to the rescue, and soon defeated the grim warder, took his keys without more ado, and opening several doors, led his companion through a labyrinth of caves until they reached a second gate guarded like the first, the warder having the body of an ass and the head of a wolf. "Who knocks at the gates of Hate?" he said fiercely.

"Love," answered the valiant fairy, waving his sword.

"Love isn't wanted here," replied the monster. "Begone! Or I will kill you both." Whereupon he opened the gate and advanced towards them; but the elfin engaged him at once, and so great was his power that he overturned the creature in a moment.

"Now, Malice, I have thee," cried the brave sprite sternly. "Yield up thy keys and get thee hence, and hide thyself, together with Envy, at the outer gate, for if I find you here on my return I will slay you both.'

Malice gave up his keys and ran howling along the rocky caverns of the place; while Love, the elfin, led the woman onward through a catacomb of dismal vapour, which ended in a series of arched chambers, draped and festooned with sheets of solid gold. The horrid creatures who inhabited the place were hideous and frightful to behold. Some had two heads, others were without legs or arms; many crawled like snakes, and not a few presented the appearance of being half man and half beast. These monsters fled in all directions at the sight of Love, and so he passed onward unmolested until he came to Cavernous Hall—the palace of Croak and Gloom—and here he found the two great chiefs of Hate with the children, Winnie and Edith. The hall was filled with the rank and fashion of the nation to see the wonderful mortals of the upper world; and into their midst walked Love and the woman hand-in-hand.

"Who are these strange people?" cried the terrible voice of Gloom, grasping the little ones in his arms, for they had uttered a glad cry at sight of their mother.

"My children! Oh, give me my children!" pleaded the woman.

"Mortal, how came you here?" inquired the grim Croak.

"It was I who guided her hither," answered the elfin.

"Then thou shalt die," exclaimed the vast throng, as with one voice.

"Not all your hosts of this dim region nor your power can destroy me. Dash me to pieces against the rugged walls of your palace, burn me to ashes, and scatter them to the vapours, still I shall rise up stronger, in some other form to give you battle. Give the woman her little ones."

"Beware! Let the race of this mortal give us back our stolen treasures. They have invaded our domain, and have rifled it of some of its richest treasures. Through soil and rock and granite they have delved down, down into this under world, until we could hear the ring of their tools. And we have seen them change our dim regions into a wilderness."

While Croak uttered these words the elfin glided swiftly forward, seized the children, and placing them safely in the mother's arms, cried hurriedly, "Begone; run to the outer gate, and my power shall bear you company and carry you swiftly to the upper air. Quick!"

And the woman, pressing her babes tightly to her throbbing bosom, fled away, and rising through the mists which obscure the lower world, regained the hut on the cliff; while Love battled with the legions of Hate, and battles with them still—ay! and will battle with them to the end of time.

# BABY'S VISITORS.

OPEN the window, wide. How serene and peaceful it is out yonder, where the stars gleam and sparkle—some faint and small as a diamond speck, others large, clear, and dazzling, as the eyes of angels gazing through the dim void earthward to that little room where Baby sleeps the sleep of death. It may have been the shadowing of that radiance, attendant on the sinless ones, whom we call angels, which had cast athwart the infant's features a sheen of glory, and changed them into the seeming of a sleeping cherub, or perchance the immortal glow that shimmered, widening and circling as it fell, was but the forerunner of that celestial band who bridge space and *suffer little children to go unto* Him!

See the mother kneeling beside her dead babe, her slender frame convulsed with agony. Not a tear, not a sob, that breaks forth for her lost darling but freights its newly awakened soul and holds it backward from the angels. How can it soar while the kindred spirit below wails its absence, and every moan shouts, trumpet tongued, "Come back! Come back!"

"It was my world," she says, "my whole world, and it has gone from me like a vision. Alas! Common things live on; earth's mighty heart still throbs! Creation lifts its voice in sea and air, and in the world's great mart. Music, life, and motion are everywhere, save in my babe."

Alas! for thee, fond mother, whose vision mounts no higher than the baby's cot. Alas! for thee!

Frail, yet beautiful, were the creatures who entered at the open window. Softly as kindly thoughts that gathered round the infant sleeper in wonder, and laid a ring of flowers about it, until they formed a rosy cradle. And then, as the sighing wind or those more delicate strains heard in dreams, the voices of the elfins rose upon the stillness of the night like silver bells.

Solemn was their chant, and weird and fanciful, which anon changed to lighter vein and measure. The mourner heard the sounds, and wondered as the cadence rose and fell upon her grief-dulled ears, but the singers were invisible to her.

"Nurslings of the summer air
    Buzz, buzz, here, there.
  So we! quaint and gay,
    Antic gambol,
      Gnome and Fay.

"Whispering to the smiling moon,
    Trill, trill, 'Come soon.'
  So we! quaint and gay,
    Antic gambol,
      Gnome and Fay.

"As the breezes come and go.
    Hum, hum. Just so.
  So we! quaint and gay,
    Antic gambol,
      Gnome and Fay."

As a single drop of water contains things with life and being, which cannot be seen with the naked eye, so in space dwell the creatures of the imagination, both wise and beautiful, being full of love and sympathy for mankind and goodwill towards women and young children. Show me a selfish, disobedient boy, or a naughty girl, who ever saw a fairy. You can't. I defy you to produce one. But many a bright youth and pretty maiden, who love truth and obedience better than play or lollies, can testify that the lovely persons who came to them in dreams were the same who now stood round the cradle of the dead baby.

How these wee people had loved it, and had

kept watch and ward over it, ever since they had espied it in its basket cradle downstairs! Fresh from the mysterious star-world, of which they knew nothing, they had marvelled at it, and had crowed and cooed and sung to it, until it had begun to know them, and answer after its fashion, and laugh, and shake its fat, dimpled fists and crow too.

How they had watched it when it slept, and filled its tiny brain with innocent visions pure as the setting sun! How they had caused their magic to mantle its slumber, and the little rosebud mouth to open out in smiles! How silent and still now! No smile parts the pale lips. Not all the witchcraft in Fairyland, nor all the songs sung by sprite or fay to fretful babyhood, can lift but even one slender hair from those drooping eyelids which shroud the dim, blue eyes.

"Baby's dead," said one, and "Dead, dead, dead," repeated all the elfin circle.

"Let us bear it hence unto the open glade. The bright beams of the morning sun will bring back its look of gladness, and we shall hear its voice again."

"Ay, bear it hence," replied the chorus.

Cradled in the wild flowers they had spread around it, the elfins carried off their silent burden, and laid it gently within a scented grove, and as the glorious morn broke forth to life and gladness, the birds gathered together in the fairy haunt and sang a requiem.

Up rose the sun and filled the dell with golden splendour. Its shining beams spread through the foliage in amber-coloured radiance, and played about the fair head of the dead baby until the creatures around shrank back in awe at the sight; but the sun brought no light to its eyes, nor smile to its lips. And so they carried the infant back again within its little room, and departed wondering.

Oh, weeping mother, whose bitter tears have drenched thy baby's winding sheet, had'st thou faith even as a grain of mustard seed in the *Master*, thou couldst see above thee, beyond that cold, dead clay, the forms of angels bearing thy little one to eternal rest.

Oh, ye parents, shall I preach to you, as well as to your children? Ye who, when your daily task is done, sit brooding o'er the loss of some fondly remembered child, now sleeping its long sleep in death, take heart if ye have loved it; then it is not dead, but lives again within you. Love cannot die, for it is as immortal as the soul. Like Jacob's ladder, it is the broad pathway from Paradise to earth, by which our little ones come back to us in visions and in dreams to give us assurance of the tender care of God.

# RUBYWINGS.

## CHAPTER I.

### THE JOURNEY.

COME with me for an hour, out of the hard, stony by-ways and hot, dusty thoroughfares of this work-a-day city.

Mount behind me on the broad wings of this carrier-bird, which most men have, yet which no mortal hath ever seen! Sit close and fear not, for our pillion is soft and easy, the steed safe. Now mount and away!

> "Where silvery songs of bird and bee,
> Of leaf and lake and stream,
> Round us hum and flit and flee
> While we linger silently
> In our noon-tide dream."

Nothing but ice! Walls of it, peaks, spires, towers, grottoes, floors. Ice everywhere! It is of all manner of delicate hues—pale green and blue; and where the edges catch the sun it shines even brighter than the glitter of a thousand clustering diamonds. This is Silverhaze, the border of Fairyland. The King of Silverhaze stood at the ice-bound portal of his kingdom, when he observed the approach of a very old man. The gait of the mortal wayfarer was slow and feeble, and he often paused to rest ere he reached the gates where stood the monarch.

"Who lives here, Spirit?" he asked of the Frost King.

"I," responded the tall, bearded form, in a sweet voice which sounded like a song heard a long way off.

"Where is Fairyland, and how am I to get there?" inquired the old gentleman in a faint tone.

"You are standing on the boundary line of the region you seek," answered the King; "this is the wall encircling the land of the Australian Elves, O mortal!"

"What a thick rampart of ice!" exclaimed the old man, curiously inspecting the great white barrier.

"True," answered the Frost King. "This wall is made from the dew and rain of Earth that are not delicate enough to moisten the tender grass of Elfland. I catch the mists as they wreathe themselves upward, and divide them; that which has touched and been tainted with the under world I build up into these icy walls; that which is pure as the morning cloud floats on into the country where you are going."

"Thank you; may I wander onward?"

"Ay! Few come here to break my repose. I live here alone. Continue your journey onwards towards Moonrise, and you will see all you want."

"Shall I see everything, O King Frost?"

"Nay, that will depend on yourself. If you can fling away from you every thought that is not fit for the pure mind of an innocent child, then shall you behold wonders."

"Alas! great King, I am afraid I cannot do that. Who can, who can? In my youth I never heard of this glorious Fairyland. Childhood, young manhood, mature age, were all spent by me in getting and hoarding money; and now the time is drawing near when I must depart; but ere I go I want to view the silver mosses and green slopes of these regions."

The old man bent low before the Ice Monarch, whose cold blue eyes changed to flashing steel.

"I can help you," he answered. "Come here, and let me touch your forehead. If you wish it in your heart, I will draw from you your memories and thoughts, and send you a child into Fairyland.

"The old man bent low before the ice monarch."

*Australian Fairy Tales.* [Page 266]

Your past will lie here for you in my ice cave, a burden or a blessing, for you to resume as you go out."

"How, a burden or a blessing?" asked the mortal.

"That again will depend on yourself; according to what you see in your travels will your *past* seem to you on your return."

"But you said I should see all."

"You will have the power of seeing all, yet you will only see that which you care to look upon. As the Frost King spoke, he advanced and touched the mortal's brow with his finger. While he did so there glided beneath the old man's feet a silver cloud-car, which instantly enveloped him and carried him away from the ice-clad border with the swiftness of a sea-gull. Amazement grew upon him as he felt himself borne away and no visible thing in view. Then remembering what the Spirit had said, he exclaimed aloud, "Can I not see what is about me?"

The words were hardly uttered when he perceived that he was the occupant of a gorgeous conveyance drawn by a team of butterflies, with a lovely child seated therein driving them. Wonderful indeed the delicate tints and shades which the moonbeams had woven in her robes. Still more wondrous the blended purity and beauty of her face. Exquisitely, deliciously soft and musical the voice that addressed him in accents like the soft south wind, wooing the trees at summer's eventide.

"Welcome, Sir Mortal. Welcome to Elfland."

"Dear child, art thou a fairy?" he cried in surprise.

"'I AM QUEEN OF THE BUTTERFLIES,' SHE REPLIED."

"Yes! My name is Rubywings," she answered, with a beaming smile.

"Rubywings," he repeated. "It is a delightful name, my child; but why do they call thee Rubywings?"

"Because I am Queen of the Butterflies," she

replied; "and because I am also the messenger of Peace and Charity to the good of the Earth. Invisible to all else of mortal birth am I. Peace! Let us onward."

Brilliantly flashed the wings of the butterflies as they wafted the cloud-car, light and joyous as the golden orioles that flew before them. Here they fluttered among curious rocks of veined and marbled stone, here and there soft mosses, which grew in little clumps, some in scales, like trays on which stood silver cups for the fays to drink out of. Then ferns peeped out with their long tresses that blew backwards and forwards in the wind. A trickle of water began to flow from a deep cranny, and tall plants blossomed along its course. Suddenly they came upon a wide, beautiful plain, robed with such lovely, silk-like grass, only to be found in these regions. Here tall palms tossed their feathery heads, while creepers, bearing flowers, streaked with gold and brown, climbed about their trunks.

Still onward, with but a passing glimpse at the emerald carpet beneath, until they reached a fine lagoon, in the midst of which an island appeared to view, so fair and beautiful that the rest of the landscape turned bleak and barren by comparison. Over this wondrous place Rubywings guided the cloud-car. Landing where a mossy bank sloped gently to the water, the fairy led her companion into such a charming garden that a burst of rapture broke from his lips at sight of it. The most refined imagination of mortal man never conceived such a world of rare beauty. No seasons came and went here, the flowers bloomed eternally. Like a jewelled crown encircling the brows of a queen, so a vast ring of pale blossoms surrounded this bower of loveliness—primrose, with her beseeching face, shy snowdrop, loving violet, with her whisper of summer, glad hyacinth, ringing a peal of bells, whose faint tinkle came upon the mortal's ears, like subdued melody.

Rubywings pointed out a soft couch of ferns, bordered with lilies, and said,—

"Rest thee here awhile, O mortal. Sleep, dream, bewilder thyself. When thou wakest, thine eyes shall open upon the ministering spirits of Nature, which I go to bring around thee.

> "'Bi baby bunting,
> I am going hunting
> For the shadows as they fly,
> For the winds to waft them by;
> Bi baby bunting!'"

Ere her childish song had ended Rubywings vanished, and the mortal fell asleep.

## CHAPTER II.

#### SHADOWS.

THE old mortal, whom the fays had christened Ready Money, slept soundly in that island garden into which he had been guided by Rubywings. And as he slumbered, behold the Fairy Queen approached with a golden wand in her hand. She stood over him and gently waved the wand to and fro, when lo! the flowers around and about instantly assumed the shape of frolicsome sprites who formed themselves into a vast ring about him. Again Rubywings lifted her enchanted staff, and the trees receded backwards in the distance as so many drifting clouds athwart the horizon. And waving her wand for the third time, a sudden darkness shrouded the island save where the man reposed.

Round that clear, circular space, bordered by the crowded ranks of the elves, there shone a brilliant, steady, silvery light, brighter than the sun and softer than a moonbeam.

Rubywings stooped and whispered in the sleeper's ear. And as she did so, the magic ring widened and widened out, until at length it appeared to encompass the whole landscape. The beautiful light increased simultaneously with the wonderful expansion of the garden, thereby adding a tenfold beauty to every object upon which it rested.

"Behold, mortal, this is the valley of the shadows. First lift thine eyes," cried the fairy.

Ready Money obeyed, and saw much clearer than with his waking sight. Into the shimmering ring there glided the Monarch of the Shadows. He was not at all black or gloomy. Not in the least—his manners were soft and engaging, and his robe was decorated with all kinds of delicate tints, brown and silver-grey, and violet shaded with faint blue and azure. All the fays bowed down reverently before him, because they knew he was the greatest Shadow in the land. Painters loved him and made charming pictures of him, and poets sang of him and wrote songs in his praise, and yet neither painter nor poet could tell how great, how magnificent and glorious he was.

Troop by troop, rank and column, the Shadows came out of the ravines, valleys and dells, and from the clefts in the hill sides, and from amongst the rocks, and approached the King in due order and gave an account of their several missions.

Some told how they had spent their time in sick rooms, where people lay tossing in pain, and how they had rested the eyes of many a weary sufferer, and shielded them from the glaring light, and how sometimes they had gathered thickly round them and lulled them into health-giving sleep. Others spoke of travellers far from home, who, longing to see their wives and children or friends once more, had been comforted by the Shadows, who took upon themselves the dear home figures and the scenes of home.

The mortal listened eagerly to every word uttered by these ministers of Nature. Hitherto he had believed that Beam and Shadow alike had no life, any more than the particles of dust beneath his feet, and were just as useless. What sick couch had *he* visited? What heart comforted? What good accomplished for the benefit of his kindred? Why, the very Shadows, dim and soulless as they were, had done more good than he had done, and Ready Money trembled as the thought came home to him. One grand fellow bent his tall form before the Shadow King and said that when the summer sun waxed hot and fierce over the Australian Continent he cast himself across the fiery pathway of the burning rays, thereby refreshing many a broiling citizen, and making cool and restful shade beneath tree and hill, and giving beauty to field and stream, by throwing lovely, translucent shadows over them, and so bringing out to full perfection the form and colour of all created things.

Then there advanced Shadows of a gloomier, darker hue. Drooping, careworn, and sorrow-laden, they had come from the houses of the very poor, from courts of justice, from prison cells where criminals sat in silence and despair. Many had come from homes where there was no love of parents; where wives and husbands were at strife; where fierce words, and cruel blows, and hard usage were the rule of daily death in life. Others had just left places of business, where men, who ought to know better, toiled year after year to increase their wealth, striving after gold, lying and cheating for it, holding it tightly when they had it, and shuddering as the time drew near when they must go hence and leave it all to others.

If these Shadows, fresh from counting-houses and cobweb-covered chambers, wherein sat men faded and wan, as the colourless walls around them, if they had been the Shadow only of this listening mortal, they could hardly have presented a more realistic picture of his life in the past than they did in their report of others.

Lying there powerless, there came upon him a strong desire to get back amongst his fellow-men if it were only for one short month—nay, but only the length of a brief day; for in it what good might be done and what atonement made! Alas! for our resolution. Ready Money was fast held beneath the influence of the wand of Rubywings, and therefore could not budge.

When the grim Shadows rested, there came an altogether merrier group upon the scene. These related how they had given their attention to schoolrooms, alarming idle boys and girls by bringing the Shadow of their teachers upon them just in the middle of a game of romps. Others again had had rare fun with naughty little folks who were going to help themselves to sugar and jam, by looking over their shoulders and making believe that *some one* was coming.

Next the house Shadows took their turn, and showed how they engaged themselves, by making pleasant figures on the floor and walls, dancing in the firelight, and playing bo-peep in the curtains on winter evenings. When all the reports were finished, the King called to the Wind to dismiss the Shadows.

Then the Wind came, and the Shadows, ere they took their departure, amused themselves as they liked best. In the most surprising manner some played leap-frog, hide-and-seek, and blindman's-buff. Others raced along the sward and up the side of the hills, like so many will-o'-the-wisps; many changing into all kinds of strange and fantastic shapes, until the silver light dimmed and died out, and the beautiful garden resumed its grandeur as before.

And a change came o'er the slumbering mortal. Slowly he opened his eyes, but the fairy with her enchanting wand was not there, nor the flowers and trees. Nothing, save the high boundary wall of ice and the white-bearded Frost King standing near.

"Resume thy earth-woven memories, O mortal!" he said in a grave, solemn tone. "Stand upright that I may touch thee. So! Go thy way for a brief season. In thy daily wanderings here and there thy former friends shall not recognise thee! From henceforth, Greed, Selfishness, Envy, and all of that nature that were dear to thee, shall become thy bitter foes. Remember what the Shadows said. Farewell!"

Down, earthward, with tottering and uncertain step went the mortal; downward, along the broad, sunny pathway, where innumerable birds sang, and trees waved, and where the low, hoarse murmur of bread-winning millions ascended to the Creator.

# LIFE AND DEATH.

ONCE upon a time an old man and a fairy sat by the wayside talking.

"When the world was first created," said the elfin, "it was appointed how many years each creature should exist. So the horse came and inquired how long he was to live.

"'Thirty years,' he was told, and then was asked, 'Is that sufficient?'

"'Alas!' replied the beast, 'that is a long time. Think how many wearisome burdens I shall have to carry from morning to night beneath a hot sun, that man, my master, may eat bread and live at ease, and I receive nothing but blows and hard words, and must yet keep always active and obliging. The time is too long. Take away some of my years, I pray.'

"So the horse was pitied, and a life of only eighteen years was appointed to him. Whereupon he went gladly away; and the dog then made his appearance and asked,—

"'What is the duration of my life?'

"'How long do you wish to live?' was inquired of him. 'Thirty years was allotted to the horse, but that was too much for him; perhaps you will be satisfied with that term?'

"'Do you think so?' answered the dog. 'Remember how much I shall have to run and bark and bite. My feet will not last the time, and when I have lost my voice and my teeth, and can neither bark nor bite, what will then be for me but to crawl and howl from one corner to another?'

"Therefore the dog's plea was granted, and twelve years appointed for his age. After which he departed and made room for the monkey.

"'You will live thirty years willingly, no doubt,' was said to the ape. 'You need not work like the horse or the dog, and therefore will always be well off.'

"'Indeed, it should be so,' replied Jacko, 'but I have found it different. Mine is anything but a life of indolence. I must always be aping my betters, and making comical faces for people to laugh at. Many a hard nut I have to crack. And as sadness is often hidden beneath a grin, so have I to show my teeth, even if they are aching with pain. Please shorten the years of my life.' So ten years were allotted to him.

"Last of all man appeared, healthy and vigorous, and requested a term to be appointed to him.

"'You shall live thirty years,' was the reply. 'Is that enough?'

"'What a short time!' exclaimed the man. 'Just when I shall have cleared my land, built myself a house, and lighted a fire upon my own hearth, and I am thinking of enjoying life, I must die. I pray let my life be lengthened.'

"'Very well. The eighteen years of the horse shall be added.'

"'That is not sufficient,' said man.

"'You shall have also twelve years of the dog's life thereto.'

"'Still too little,' replied the man.

"'Then you may have the ten years allowed to the monkey, but you must desire no more.'

"Man was then obliged to leave, but he was not satisfied.

"Thus man lives seventy years. The first thirty are the days of his manhood, which pass quickly away; he is then strong and lusty, works with pleasure, and rejoices in his being. Then follow the eighteen years of the life of the horse which brings in its train burdens which he must bear from the rising to the setting of the sun, and wherein blame and abuse often reward him for his labours. Next come the twelve years of the dog, during which man has to sit in corners, because he has lost the power to bark and bite. And when this time is up the ten years of the monkey bring the close of the scene, for in these man becomes foolish, gabbers and jabbers without end, and is fit for nothing but——"

The elfin paused, and gazed earnestly at the mortal.

"But what?" cried the old man.

"But—Death. The portal which leads into the *vast unknown*, and from which we elves are debarred," responded the fairy.

"And what is Death?"

"A certainty, O mortal, for all thy race. No more or less than that. Ere I go hence from thee for ever hear this fable:—

"In olden times a giant wrestled with this terrible enemy Death, and vanquished him. As the grim foe lay helpless by the wayside he began to grumble. 'What will be the consequence of my downfall to the world? If I lie here, then it will be so full and crowded with humanity that they will not be able to move for each other.'

"Just then a young man came up the road, strong and healthy, singing a song, and looking well about him. As soon as he perceived the conquered one he went up to him, and compassionately raising him, bound up his wounds, and nursed him until strength returned.

"'Do you know who I am?' asked Death, when he was fairly on his legs again.

"'No,' replied the youth. 'I know you not.'

"'I am Death,' he replied. 'I spare no one, and can take no excuse from you even. But to show you that I am not ungrateful, I promise not to take you unawares, but I will send my messengers before I come and fetch you.'

"'Very well,' said the young man, 'that is a bargain. Until your harbingers come I shall be safe from you.'

"With this understanding the mortal pursued his way merrily, and lived in prosperity for some time; but youth and health will not remain for ever. Pain and sickness and grief came, and the man complained that there was no rest for him night or day. 'I shall not die,' he said, 'for Death must first send his messengers; but I wish these fearful days of illness were over.'

"Health returned again, and he began to live as usual. One day, somebody knocked at the window, and looking round he saw Death standing behind him. 'Follow me,' he said.

"'How so?' exclaimed the mortal. 'Will you

break the promise that you made to me, that your servants should first give me notice ere you appeared? I have not seen them.'

"'Be silent,' replied Death. 'Have I not sent you one messenger after another? Did not fever come and seize you and lay you prostrate? Did not racking pain oppress your limbs, noises sound in your ears, a dimness cover your eyes? Above all, did not my twin brother, Sleep, remind you every night that I should come?'

"And the man knew not what to reply, and was therefore taken away."

When the elfin had thus spoken he vanished from the mortal's view.

# GIANTS.

I, MARTIN CROWE, am a book-loving vagabond. Reading hath charms for me not to be found in men or women. My few quaint volumes are my companions and my friends. True, I cannot borrow money from, or use them according to my worldly necessity; nevertheless, they speak to me in many voices, some in tones of deep wisdom, others in the witchery of suggestive imagery, until my humble study, with its scanty furniture and bare walls, vanish altogether from my outward senses.

It is late. On this long winter night I have been deep into the pages of the famous astronomer, Newton; and although I have laid down the book before me on the table, my mind is still busy at the threshold of the mysterious realm of Nature, to which I have been introduced by the wand of the magician. If knowledge is power, it sometimes happens that the power does not bring happiness in its train, but often assumes strange shapes.

As I sat and looked with vacant eyes at what, for the moment, I saw not, behold the table before me became gradually luminous. At first the light was flickering and uncertain, rising and falling in a shapeless mass, but it quickly brightened into a spiral-shaped luminary, which presently assumed the form of a venerable old man.

I cannot venture an opinion as to the means employed by my strange visitor for his entrance into my chamber, any more than you can explain to me the manifestations of clairvoyance and electro-biology.

From the first appearance of the light, and during the subsequent gradations which qualified my vision to discover a personage with the aspect of a seer of the olden time standing at my side, I have no clear idea of anything save that of being held by an all-powerful spell towards him. I had studied animal magnetism, and curative mesmerism under Tom Buckland, and knew a thing or two with reference to passes, currents, and counter-currents, but I found my will ebbing away before the steady fingers and calm eyes of the stranger, whose stronger influence seemed to wrap me round and round as with a band of steel, utterly powerless to speak or move, except at the will of my companion. Yet I felt my sensations in rapid play to all around me. Nay, more, the sense of hearing and observation seemed marvellously quickened within me, and the intensity of thought brightened from the gross element which had previously partially obscured it. The shape found voice, and addressed me:—

"Young man, I am the guardian of Nature's chief secrets," it said, replying to the unasked question on my lip. "Men call me Knowledge, but my name is Science. What dost thou want with me?"

I found the power of speech return to me ere the last words were uttered.

"Let me behold some of Nature's secrets," I cried eagerly.

"Thou art a bold mortal."

"I am earnest. Even as the aspiring thoughts that meet me in this book, I would soar and know."

"Of course," replied the voice. "Although I come to thee in fairy form and guise, I am the servant of thought. It was not the uttered word that did summon me, but the force of the inward wish to understand within thee. Well, I am here. If thou wouldst see some of the giants of the future, follow me."

I had no will but to follow him, as he led the way out of the doorway into the silent night, under the whispering trees beyond the city, across the bridge of the river, and away to the summit of a hill, with the waves of the gulf thundering at its base.

"All human knowledge commences in dreams," he said in a low tone. "Trance hovers over measureless secrets, and forms the first faint bridge between them and thought. Look steadfastly on the moon yonder."

I obeyed in silence. I had no power otherwise than to obey. As I gazed, the pale orb of night appeared to expand and dilate until its luminous circumference diffused all space, and in the midst of this shining atmosphere I became aware of a strange sense of heavenly liberty pervading my whole being. It seemed as if hitherto I had been bound with a strong chain, which had suddenly snapped asunder, and had yielded me unutterable freedom from the body, and had imparted a bird-like lightness which floated me into space itself. Through this space a swift succession of shadowy landscapes rolled; mountains, trees, cities, ships, and inland seas glided along, like the drifting clouds seen in a stormy sky, until at length, settled and stationary, I saw a vast cave in the heart of a gloomy forest.

"Enter, and beware of Fear," cried the voice at

my side. At the sound the ecstasy and lightness which had been upon me faded away, and a sort of languor seized my frame, without communicating itself to the mind.

Downward by a stairway of rugged rock I was led into what seemed a terrible abyss. Round and round in spiral form we descended for many miles, amid noises loud and new to me, when our farther progress was abruptly stopped by a massive door formed in the solid rock, and which was guarded by monsters of various shapes, called Ignorance. Erect and threatening they rose to crush me, but at sight of my conductor they fell down again in abject submission and opened the door; whereupon we passed into a mighty cavern, so wide and so lofty that its magnitude astounded me, its limit reaching far beyond my range of vision. Here I beheld huge giants, mightier than ever appeared in legend or fairy tale. Many were toiling hard, some lay reclining, as if just awakened from a deep sleep; while others slumbered peacefully. Dim and indistinct as the light here glimmered, I could see the ponderous shapes plainly. With the will to question my guide came the power of speech.

"Who is yonder fellow," I asked, "seated astride the trident rock? What huge limbs he has!"

"That is young Australia," replied the voice. "The ages have cradled him. He is only a baby awakened out of his first sleep. I predict the infant will develop into a magnificent giant by-and-by," rejoined the voice.

"What is the name of this powerful-looking creature here with the gigantic head?" I inquired, pointing to a monster who seemed but just awakened from a long nap.

"Electricity. It is a name but little known as yet," replied the sage, "but your children will see this new land filled with its wonders. You see the giant has only been disturbed, not awakened."

"Why do they not rouse him up to action, O wise sage?"

"Because the time for him to use his great and varied powers has not come," answered the voice gravely. "Powers wrested from Nature for the benefit of mankind may be also turned into a scourge for the innocent. A Titan war is waging ever among men, the good for ever on the defensive, the bad for ever in assault. Perchance 'tis well the giant sleeps."

"There is another giant standing near Electricity, whose proud look I have often noted on the faces of men I have met. Who is he?"

"He is called Money, otherwise Cash, often Hard Cash," replied the voice in answer. "Truly he is a powerful fellow. Sometimes great and god-like in his liberality, at other times he is mean and selfish. Mark what an affinity between him and the prostrate monster. In the far-off future, I see them hand-in-hand together, working a wonderful change on the face of Nature and in the condition of mankind." A faint smile passed across the features of the sage as he uttered the words.

"One question more. Pray tell me the name of yon noble creature who seems as though he were able to prop the globe single-handed?"

"Ah, that is the twin brother of young Australia, and his name is Enterprise," added the voice proudly. "Up and doing, early and late, ever active and daring in speculation. Australian Enterprise has promised that this, his country, shall be the commercial focus of the earth some time in the future, which shall also uprouse these slumbering giants."

The voice ceased speaking; but another voice, well known to my waking ears as that of my landlady, filled the vacuum, with the following choice sentence :—

"Mr. Crowe, I hopes you remember that I'm a

widder with five innercent children to keep, and can't afford to let you fall asleep and burn every drop of ile out of the lamp for a guinea a week, washing included! There now!"

# THE KANGAROO HUNTER.

## CHAPTER I.

### THE LOST DRESS.

HIS hut stood on the border of a vast and unknown tract of bushland, away north. Why he had removed from all traces of his fellows to lead such a lonely mode of life we cannot pretend to explain. All we know is that he was a tall, handsome young fellow, and known to a few of the out-station boundary riders as Bob, the Kangaroo Hunter.

One day Bob had chased a fine old man kangaroo that he had wounded farther than usual into the trackless depths of the bush. As he was returning homeward along the margin of a small lagoon he perceived an article of very fine linen lying on the sand. Our hero came to a dead halt, and stared at the article in question, with as much astonishment as if a white elephant had presented itself in his path. He took up the linen, and the more he examined it the more puzzled he became at the discovery. Bob was a capital shot, and could track game like a blackfellow, but the finding of a piece of soft cambric in such a solitary region bothered him completely. After supper he sat and thought over it, but gave it up by-and-by and went to bed.

Somewhere in the dead of night the hunter was awakened by a voice calling him by name. He could not see anything, for it was quite dark, but he felt as if it were some one moving up and down over his bunk, and at the same time a soft, gentle voice repeated, "Bob! Bob! Bob!"

"Here I am," he answered. "What do you want?"

"Please give me back—my—my—dress," replied the voice in hesitating tones.

"Eh? what?" cried our hero, sitting up and rubbing his eyes. "What did you say? *Your dress?*"

"If you please," continued the voice pleadingly, "the article you found on the shore of the lake yesterday—it is mine. Pray return it to me."

"Oh!" said Bob, "why, *that* was a lady's——"

"I know it," rejoined the voice quickly. "Oh dear. It is mine. I am a lady."

"Pray wait one moment, madam, and I will strike a light."

"It is useless. You cannot see me, I am invisible," replied the voice.

"Indeed!" ejaculated Bob, "that is a pity. However, I will return to you what I found upon one condition."

"What condition?"

"Tell me who you are."

"Alas! I am the daughter of a mighty chief, whose race and dominions are far beyond the 'Lubra Mountains,' but I have fallen into the power of a wicked magician, who has confined me on the highest summit of the Granite Cliff. Every day I am allowed to bathe in the lake accompanied by an old hag called Mother Growl; but I cannot return without my—my—dress. Yesterday I was obliged to stay by the lake, and I'm afraid the cruel witch will kill me if I'm detained here much longer."

The low, plaintive voice touched the heart of our hero, who replied, "Rest easy, poor child. Here is your garment. Yet ere you depart tell me if I can help you out of the hands of your enemies."

"Can you climb the Granite Cliff, which is as steep and smooth as a polished rod of steel? You cannot. Farewell!"

"Stop! Where there's a will there's a way,"

said Bob. "With your permission, I mean to try and do it; but I never heard of the Granite Cliff. Where is it?"

"The path lies beyond the lake towards the plains," answered the voice. "Yet do not attempt to go, for there are horrid birds and beasts who will devour you. More I dare not tell you." So saying, the voice died away in the stillness of the night. The warning uttered by the voice, instead of deterring the young hunter from approaching the dreadful cliff, only made him the more determined to make an effort to rescue the lady from her thraldrom. At the break of day he arose and loaded his gun, slung his pouch—containing powder and ball—over his shoulder, put some food in his bag, and started off for the lagoon. He traversed the country beyond the lake for some considerable distance without meeting a living thing and, feeling hungry, seated himself beneath the shade of a large tree to eat his dinner. He had not been seated many minutes when a gigantic bird alighted overhead and eyed him with some attention. Bob observed it was as big in the body as an emu, with broad wings, long beak, and talons like an eagle. Our hero had seized his gun for a shot, but he dropped the weapon as the bird called out in a hoarse tone,—

"Hello! Who are you?"

The hunter was dumb with surprise, but at length found voice to reply, "I'm a traveller."

"Oh, and what are you eating?" said the bird.

"Kangaroo," answered Bob, smiling.

"I'm very fond of kangaroo. Can I dine with you?"

"'WHAT KIND OF BIRD ARE YOU?'"

"Certainly," replied our hero; "come down and I'll share with you."

The strange bird did not wait for the invitation to be repeated. In a very short time he devoured the lion's share of the lunch, and he and our hero became very friendly.

"What kind of bird are you?"

"I'm a gum-hawk," cried he, stretching his huge wings. "We are the giants of the feathered tribe hereabouts."

"You are a monster," responded Bob in admiration. "I suppose you are quite strong enough to carry a man like me?"

"I'd carry two such as you," answered the gum-hawk quietly. "Only try me."

"Perhaps I may," said Bob. "Do you know a place named the Granite Cliff?"

"Rather; are you going there?"

"Yes," answered Bob, "if I may depend on you to convey me so far."

"Of course I will, with pleasure; one good turn deserves another. Get on my back," and ere our hero knew what he was about the bird rose with him into the blue void high above the tree-tops. Bob held on tightly, but without feeling at all alarmed at his dangerous position. From his elevated post he had a splendid view of the surrounding country. Far ahead in the distance he beheld a colossal peak, standing darkly out above the surrounding hills. Its sides were almost upright, and shone in the sun like polished marble.

"What mountain is that yonder?" he inquired of the gum-hawk.

"Mountain! That is the Granite Cliff."

"I have a large piece of kangaroo still left in my pouch," rejoined the hunter after a pause. "The meat shall be yours if you set me down on the summit of the cliff."

"Don't go there," answered the gum-hawk in a warning voice.

"Why?"

"Because it is the home of wicked people, who will kill you."

"I have no fear on that head. Will you have the meat?"

"Certainly, if you are determined," and the friendly bird, finding that our hero was resolved, flew to the apex of the rock, and there left him.

The summit appeared quite different to what one would have imagined it to be from the plain. It seemed to the eyes of Bob a small island in itself. There was a wide, clear space whereon stood an old stone house, and before its door a very large water-hole, and behind a dark belt of dense bush, which almost obscured the setting sun.

The young hunter saw neither man nor beast; all was still, save the noise of the wind among the trees, while close above his head the clouds were rolling along.

Bob stepped up to the door of the hut and

gave it a hard thump with his gun. Immediately an old woman with red eyes and a brown face opened it. She had goggles upon her nose, and looked at him sharply before she asked him how he came there.

"A gum-hawk took me up in his talons and dropped me upon this mountain," responded Bob readily.

"Well, what do you want here?"

"Entrance, my supper, and a night's lodgings, dame."

"That you shall have, but you will have to earn what you get here by difficult work on the morrow."

"I am prepared," said Bob.

"Very well. Come in," she cried, and immediately closed the door.

## CHAPTER II.

### QUIZ.

THERE was nothing extraordinary within the house on the Granite Cliff. If Dame Growl had any suspicions with reference to the visit of our hero, she kept them to herself. Bob was provided with a good supper, and a bed afterwards, where he slept as sound as a cockroach until the morning. The sun had hardly begun to peep over the top of the mountain, however, when the old woman shook him roughly by the arm. "Get up, you sluggard!" she cried. "You don't remain here and eat idle bread; you must work—work!"

"All right, dame," responded Bob cheerfully. "I'm not afraid of work in any shape."

The witch laughed grimly, thereby disclosing her black, ugly teeth. "Oh, you are a wonderful fellow, but we can match you here; we'll make you work—work!"

She hobbled off into an adjoining room, and returned with an old battered thimble, which she held out on her skinny forefinger. "Here, take this," she cried. "Now go, and empty the water-hole out there."

"What! with a thimble?" cried Bob.

"Yes; and you must finish your task before evening; also take out all the small fish, and range them according to their species on the bank. Do you hear?"

"Of course, good dame. Anything besides?" asked the hunter with bitter irony.

Mother Growl disclosed her teeth at him in answer, and left him to his toil.

Poor Bob stared at the water-hole for a good half-hour, without seeing what his gaze rested on. He had expected some reasonable work, but here he was set to do an impossibility. The hole was a very large one; almost as wide as the mouth of a river. How then was he to bale it out with a thimble? It appeared very absurd; nevertheless, our hero was determined to try. He began his work, but he found it labour in vain. When noonday came he stopped, and sat down to rest. "It's quite hopeless for me to try and empty out all this water to-day. Why, it would take me a thousand years to do it at this rate," he cried, raising his voice. "Indeed, I don't see the use of making a fuss about it; it will be the same whether I work or not. I wonder where the witch has hid that lady that came to my hut?" And with this new turn to his thoughts Bob sat by the water-hole and made circles in the water with the pebbles at his feet.

As he sat there and shied the stones into the water-hole, he heard some one cry out as if in sudden pain! Bob stared around and about him, but he could see no one.

"Oh dear! you have struck me on the head!" exclaimed a voice.

The hunter rose quickly to his feet. "Who and what are you?" he cried.

"Can't you see who I am? Look here, on the water," repeated the voice.

Our hero turned his gaze in the direction indicated, and beheld a large frog swimming towards him.

"Pray who are you, sir?" inquired Bob, filled with amazement.

"I'll tell you that presently," responded the frog, as he crawled up the embankment. He was a fine, speckled fellow with a big head, long arms and legs, and a considerable paunch, which showed that he was fond of his food.

"I was just taking my usual mid-day bath when my ears caught your reproaches with respect to emptying this lake," said the frog, at the same time bowing very politely to Bob. "May I ask if you seriously intend to attempt the task?"

The young hunter briefly explained the whole circumstances of the case.

Froggy listened quietly, and then replied, "Be content. I will help you."

"How can a frog help any one?" cried Bob contemptuously.

"Wait and see. I am not a frog as you suppose. This skin is a bathing dress, nothing more. They are very fashionable in Elfland at present. Of course the robe is not elegant, but it is comfortable. How do you like it?"

"Are you a fairy?" inquired Bob, not heeding the last remark.

"I am that. Everybody round here knows Quiz the Sprite. I'm Quiz."

"Ah! I'm sorry that stone hit you on the head."

"Never mind. It didn't hurt me much," answered Quiz. "Now allow me to help you with your task."

"Can you really help me?"

"Certainly. Old Dame Growl is no friend of mine; and I have those with me who can execute any tasks she may find for you to do, no matter how difficult they may be."

As Quiz spoke, he opened his speckled covering, and out stepped three little men, no bigger than one's thumb. The first was slim and slender, with a very resolute face, the other two were strong and robust.

"These creatures may appear to you quite insignificant," continued the sprite, "but they are not so. Stand aside and watch what this, the smallest of them, can do." Saying which Quiz made a sign for Bob to retire a few paces; which he did.

"Now, Resolute, give us a taste of your quality, by emptying out that water-hole," cried Quiz.

Ere the words had left the elfin's mouth the

wee man advanced, and said, "Out, water—out, fishes," and immediately the water rose in the air like a white vapour, and rolled away with the other clouds; while the fish all jumped out and arranged themselves on the bank according to their size and species.

"Well done, Resolute!" shouted Bob, in ecstasy.

"Dame Growl will set you harder tasks to-morrow than this one," resumed the sprite. "Yet keep good heart, and I will help you to accomplish them and to rescue the chief's lovely daughter from her hands. To-morrow I shall see you again."

And with another polite bow, Quiz gathered the wee little men beneath his skin, and hopped away to a deep crevice in the cliff, where he vanished from sight.

When evening fell the Witch came forth from the house leaning on her staff.

"Ah, sluggard!" she cried, "if you have not done the work I gave you I will have you thrown head-foremost from the cliff."

Bob laughed, and pointed with his finger to the lines of fishes and the wide, empty water-hole.

Dame Growl held her skinny arms aloft in amazement.

"Who has done this task for you?" she shouted

in unbridled passion. "Tell me who it was, and I'll have them boiled, roasted, and baked for my husband's dinner."

"I sha'n't tell you anything, dame," answered Bob. "You gave me a job to do; there it is done, according to order, and now I want my supper, please."

The old woman looked silently and maliciously at him for several minutes, and then replied, "Very well, very well; doubtless you are a wonderful fellow; but I have a task in store for you to-morrow which will tax all your cleverness to accomplish. You got off too easily to-day. Wait till to-morrow."

Bob followed her as she went towards the hut, muttering under her breath and shaking her staff at some imaginary foe. He ate his supper, like a man who was hungry, and then retired to rest for the night.

## CHAPTER III.

### A SLEEPING BEAUTY.

WHEN morning dawned, the enchantress conducted Bob to that belt of trees before mentioned and which was situated to the rear of the hut. "See here, my son," she said, with a wicked leer, which made her face look positively odious; "your task to-day will be to cut down every tree on the cliff—split and cut the timber into short lengths; then you must pile the whole into one great stack, so that we may have a beacon to light the night hereabouts."

"Is that all?" answered Bob, with self-feigned contempt. "Why, dame, I could stand on my head and do all that."

She shot another evil glance at him from beneath her shaggy brows. "I care not how you stand," she replied, "only the work I have given you must be finished before evening. You came here on a very foolish errand, but you do not return without your lesson."

"What errand, dame?"

"To rescue my prize. The maiden who lost her robe, eh?"

"The lady is here, then?"

'Ay, and likely to remain here, foolish boy," she cried. "Get to work—get to work. Faint heart never won fair lady. Ho! Ho! Hi! Hi!" With these words she gave him an axe, wedges, and a mallet, then hobbled away to the hut.

Bob gazed after her with a confident smile on his handsome face. "None but the brave deserve the fair," cried he as he set to work at his task;

but at the first blow he discovered that his axe was only lead, and also that the wedges were made of tin.

"This is too hard," he muttered angrily. "The affair with the thimble was bad enough, but this promises to become a trifle more interesting. What's to be done now? I can't fell trees with a leaden axe, or split logs with tin wedges, that's certain. Well, I may as well take it easy till the fairy comes; he'll help me out of it all right." With this philosophical view of things our hero stretched himself full length beneath a huge gum to await his friend.

The morning had become intensely hot and sultry, therefore it was much more pleasant in the shade than felling trees in the full glare of the sun. So Bob thought, as the morning waned apace, and the heat grew more intense. Noontide found the young hunter still reclining in the shade, and not a tree down. If they had given him a proper set of tools he could have made a start at all events; as it was, he could only strain his eyes looking for Quiz to make his appearance, and he was growing tired even of that. Try as he would, he could not keep from nodding. The deep stillness, the oppressive heat, together with that low, buzzing, sleep-producing sound of insect life, appeared to draw down his eyelids as if each of them had been freighted with a four-pound weight. In the midst of his torpor, however, Bob felt a sharp pinch on his leg. Looking up, the first thing upon which his gaze rested was a very tiny lady dressed all in red. Close by stood a magnificent little carriage, from which the lady had evidently just alighted. Such a small, funny conveyance Bob had never seen before. It was constructed entirely of wild flowers, and drawn by six well-matched locusts, in lieu of ponies, with a butterfly for a coachman. By the side of the latter Bob recognised the two little men whom he had seen with Quiz the sprite.

"Pray, what are you doing here?" inquired the small lady in shrill tones.

"Alas, madam," replied Bob, "I came here to attempt the rescue of a lovely maiden, who is under the spell of Dame Growl, the witch of this cliff."

"Ah! And why do you not rescue the lady, instead of slumbering away your time here?" cried the fairy.

"Indeed, dear lady, the power of the enchantress can only be broken by the performance of certain very difficult tasks, which I am quite unable to perform without help."

"What will you give me if I aid you?" inquired the tiny lady.

"Twenty kisses," answered Bob promptly.

"Agreed! I'll take the kisses first," she said, with a rosy blush.

The pair of wee men on the box turned away their heads while our hero paid his hire, and the gaudy coachman got down from his perch to adjust the traces which had caught round one of the leader's legs.

After what had happened, it appeared quite natural for Bob to hand the lady to her carriage, and, still further, to accompany her along the opposite side of the rock, chatting, smiling, and nodding pleasantly by the way until the butterfly coached the team down a broad cleft that formed an avenue to a small cave.

The tiny lady conducted the young hunter within; where he beheld one of the most lovely damsels lying asleep upon a marble couch. The sleeper seemed so divinely beautiful, that our hero stood speechless with admiration.

"Here slumbers the beauty whom you seek," she said.

"How lovely!" responded Bob, clasping his hands together. "I will awaken her."

"Nay, you cannot," replied the fairy. "While

the witch lives this fair, innocent maiden will remain under the spell of the enchantment."

"Let us go and kill the witch," urged Bob.

"Hush! That would be a worse crime still. Have patience yet a little while. Dame Growl will be punished ere long, and by the very means she has devised for your overthrow. And now be good enough to follow those two mannikins to the place where I met you. They are brave workers, and will soon accomplish your task. When it is finished, return hither with them."

At a sign from her the wee men departed, followed by the young hunter, who marvelled at the beauty of the sleeping maiden.

Since the days when our sturdy forefathers cleared the land to build their huts, the sun had never looked down on such extraordinary tree-felling as that which the two dwarfs began on the Granite Cliff. From the point where Bob stood, it appeared as if innumerable giants were at work. Crash! crash! crash! was heard on all sides; and, still more wonderful, to note that the trees were no sooner down than they seemed to roll asunder to the desired lengths, and to split without the aid of mallet or wedges, and then to hop away like so many imps and lay themselves into a vast heap.

Long before the evening our hero saw the task

completed; but the dwarfs had not finished yet. With the same amazing despatch they gathered together all the dry leaves and the dead timber, and piling these against the stock, they set fire to the whole mass.

It was not long ere a mighty conflagration arose which wrapped the apex of the mountain in a sheet of fire. The forked tongues shot upward to the clouds, and across the space where the house stood, until it was seen as in the midst of a furnace.

The hunter hastened back to the cave when the flames began to ascend. As he reached the place, a great shock seemed to rend the cliff asunder.

"What is that?" he cried.

"It is the death of the wicked enchantress, Dame Growl," answered the wee lady. "The fire has enfolded her in its embrace, and so her power is at an end. See! the sleeping beauty is awakening from the spell."

While the fairy uttered the words, Bob saw the maiden stretch out her shapely arms and fold them about her golden locks, and at the same time she sighed deeply.

"Approach, mortal," continued the fay, with a smile. "Touch her lips with thine, so shall it rouse her into waking life; for upon whom her bright eyes shall first rest there will her love take root and abide for ever."

And the youth kissed the budding, rosy mouth, and as he did so, behold! there opened to his gaze a vision of Paradise.

# THE LAUGHING JACKASS.

## CHAPTER I.

### LOST IN THE BUSH.

"HA-HA-HA! Ho-ho-ho!" roared the laughing jackass. It was a glorious morning in the heart of the bush. The warm sun glinted athwart the branches of the trees and cast festoons of light beneath, as if some gigantic magic lantern was at work.

The mocking bird of Australia sat perched upon the highest bough of a giant red-gum and looking down beneath upon the form of a wee urchin lying prostrate on the turf, sobbing as if his little heart was breaking.

"Ha-ha-ha! Ho-ho-ho!" laughed the merry jackass, making the bushland ring again with its mimic jeers.

The boy under the tree ceased sobbing and looked up. "It's a fine thing to laugh when one's in trouble," he said, espying the long ugly beak of the scoffer pointing down towards him. "I'll bet if I only had my Shanghai I'd soon make you laugh t'other side of your mouf."

"Ho-ho-ho!" chuckled the jackass in reply.

"Oh, it's no use troubling about a silly bird, muttered the child sadly. "*He* can't help me. Oh, I wish he could!" And the sobbing recommenced more intensely than before.

Poor Berty Wake was lost in the bush—lost utterly. For two whole days the child had wandered on and on hoping to find his way back again to that section on the back blocks which his father farmed and where he had been born. For two days the child had not seen a sign of civilisation, nor any form of life whatsoever, save a native bear, one or two wallabies, and this mocking jackass, who seemed to add to the poor wanderer's grief by its unseemly laughter.

Berty, who was one of five brothers, had been sent early in the morning, by his father, to hunt up an old roan mare, who had a great love for straying away in the bush. The boy had been diligent in his search, but could find no trace of the pony anywhere; and when he began to track back home again night came on, and the boy found he was astray in the trackless waste, with not a single point or landmark to guide him.

Poor Berty! how he coo-eed and called on his mother and his father, and then cried himself to sleep under the big gum-trees, and when daylight came again walked on and on, bravely hoping to find the track to guide him home again. No use though. Here he was the beginning of the third day, tired and hungry and much deeper in the lonesome wilderness than before.

"Ho-ho-ho!" laughed the jackass.

"If I only had something to eat—just a piece of bread—wouldn't it be nice!" said the lost one, sighing ruefully.

"Or a mince-pie!" cried a voice from the tree-top.

Berty Wake jumped to his feet. "Who's that?" he cried.

"Ho-ho-ho!" laughed the jackass hoarsely.

"Who spoke?" repeated the child, with an hysterical sob; "please say that again—mince-pie, wasn't it?"

"And jam tart," added the voice again, but sounding much nearer than before.

Poor Berty clapped his tiny hands in delight. "Ah! It's some one come at last," he cried.

"Yes, Berty Wake, it's me!" gurgled the bird in a deep, guttural tone, at the same time dropping down on a broad limb of the tree just over the

# THE LAUGHING JACKASS.

boy's head. "Here am I, Jack the Rover—otherwise, Laughing Jack, as my pa calls me."

For fully a minute the boy stood gaping at the strange bird, too much astonished to utter a word.

"Was it—was it really you who talked just now?" he said, with a quaver of fear in his voice.

"'YOU CAN'T BE OUR JACK?'"

"Why, of course it was," said the jackass, whetting his beak in a reflective way and shaking his huge head to and fro.

"Oh!" cried Berty, "I know you can laugh and whistle, but I didn't know you could talk. Where did you learn?"

"In a cage on the Murray River," replied the bird, laughing loudly. "I belonged to a squatter named Wake—Stephen Wake. He took me out of a nest when I was a wee urchin like you and taught me all I know."

"Good gracious! Why, you can't be our Jack?" cried Berty joyfully.

"That's just what I am; Jack the Rover. Ha-ha-ha! Ho-ho-ho!" replied the bird, ruffling his feathers in great glee. "Ever since my wings have grown I have taken flights from the station when it suited me. Yesterday, I heard you were lost in the bush; so I came after you on my own account, and found you asleep under this tree."

"You are a very kind fellow, Jack," said poor Berty with tears in his eyes and in his voice.

"Not half so kind as you have often been to me, my boy," replied the bird gravely. "Don't you remember when Tom nearly broke my legs with the bullock hobbles how you nursed and fondled me, and gave me tit-bits of sugar and cream, and hid me in the stable loft until I was well again? Ho-ho-ho!"

"It is wonderful," cried the child, with wide-open astonished eyes.

"Not at all. There is nothing wonderful in kindness, Berty Wake. That is natural. The wonderful part lies in *gratitude*, my dear. Gratitude moved me to find you, if you were alive. Now here we are."

Little Berty laughed, and the bird followed suit with interest.

"I suppose you are hungry?" said the bird.

"Please don't mention it," responded the wee fellow, with wistful look. "You haven't really a mince-pie anywhere about, have you?"

"Haven't I though!" answered Jack, with his hoarse laugh. "Just be good enough to follow me over to yonder peak. I'll show you." Saying which, Jack the Rover alighted on the ground, hopping in very stately fashion towards the spot indicated, our little hero following.

Halting before the hollowed trunk of a huge tree, the bird began to scatter a mound of leaves within the cone, and lo! there came to view three lovely pies.

"Sit down, Berty, and eat," said the jackass. "You'll find them very fresh and nice. I took them from the larder at the station yesterday, while your father and brothers were out hunting for you."

"Oh, I shall be glad to get back home again, Jack."

"That's all right. There's such a lot of people

out after you, but they won't find you, Berty. Jack the Rover shall have the pleasure of guiding you home again."

"Come here, Jack, and let me kiss you," said the child. "Won't you?"

"Ha-ha-ha! The idea. You can't kiss with your mouth full of pie. Besides, what will the trees say?"

"The trees. Can they know?" cried the boy, with surprise.

"Can't they!" said Jack the Rover confidently. "The trees talk to me. Listen! Don't you hear them—the rustling of the leaves against each other in the breeze? That is how they talk."

"And can you understand what they say, Jack?"

"Of course I can, Berty. They are whispering something to me now. Something that I want to know very much."

"Tell me what they say, Jack."

"They say that you must sit here beneath their protecting shade and finish your pies," said the bird solemnly. "If you stir from beneath these trees before I return, you will be totally lost to those you love, and die a dreadful death in the bush."

"Are you going to leave me, Jack?"

"Only for a short time," said the bird assuringly. "Finish your repast, and wait patiently till I return. I won't be long away." Saying which the laughing jackass mounted on the wing and was soon lost to view.

## CHAPTER II.

### EMU ROYAL.

BERTY WAKE sat under the trees and waited. Around him rose gigantic ridges of bare rock, rent and torn in quaint shapes, representing towers, peaks, and spires; riven cliffs, dells, moss-grown and webbed and festooned with finest drapery of ferns and wild flowers.

It seemed a long time to the anxious child, straining his eyes, watching for the return of the friendly jackass. Then in utter weariness the little watcher became drowsy, his heavy eyelids closed, and he slept.

How long he remained asleep he could not tell. Something touched his face and he awoke.

Standing before him he saw a fine, strong emu —full-grown, with a soft crimson saddle fixed between its wings, and a bridle on its head and round its beak glittering with precious stones.

The boy rubbed his eyes to make certain he was awake, and touched the huge bird with his finger. The talking jackass seemed commonplace in comparison with this wonderful picture. However, Berty had little time to indulge in his astonishment, for Jack the Rover, from the thick branches of the tree, commanded him to mount the curious steed.

"I can't ride an emu. I shall fall off," cried poor Berty in some alarm.

"Why, I thought an Australian could ride anything," echoed the jackass, with a loud peal of laughter. "Don't be afraid, my little man: Emu Royal is a safe animal and warranted not to buck."

Emu Royal bowed in a stately way at the compliment, and Berty Wake, over-coming his surprise, caught hold of the silken reins and sprang upon its back.

"Ha-ha-ha! Ho-ho-ho! Isn't it funny?" laughed the jackass from the tree-top. "Now on we go. I'll lead the way, and do you follow me, Emu Royal. Quick march!"

No bush-bred horse ever sped over the ground so easily and speedily as Emu Royal. At first poor Berty had some difficulty in keeping his seat, the mode of transit was so queer and unusual, but he soon became accustomed to the long swinging stride of the gigantic bird, who seemed to know his way through the intricate windings of the scrub without any aid whatever from Jack the Rover; for that knowing blade sailed smoothly on the wing high overhead, and appeared to have no other purpose in life than to scare the young parrots from their nests with his demoniacal laughter.

They went swiftly along, every bump and jolt and bound of the strange steed seemed to say, "Berty Wake's going home. The lost is found—Berty's coming home."

Hills and plains, lakes, and forests of trees appeared and went by them like a drifting cloud.

Then, suddenly, they emerged into a quiet dell, ringed in by tall gum-trees, where the grass was emerald green, and soft to the tread as a carpet of velvet pile. Here, without the least warning, the emu gave a sudden spring in the air, and lightly deposited our little hero on the broad of his back on the sward; and before Berty was aware of what had happened, Emu Royal had vanished from his sight.

The boy rose to his feet and looked about him; there was no one in view, not even the laughing jackass. *Then he laughed* in childish glee and clapped his hands.

"Why, this is Fir Tree Hollow," he said, half laughing, half crying. "Don't I know every bush and sapling in it? And there's the sheep track leading to the river, and the dray road that winds round the back of our fence. Why, I'm at home again. Coo-ee! Coo-ee!!"

A reply came to his call in the shape of a shrill neigh from a neighbouring copse.

"Gracious me! That's our old mare. I know her dear old whinny out of a hundred. Coo-ee!"

And the child ran scampering off, and came forth presently, leading by the forelock a roan quadruped which showed ample signs of recognition.

"Where have you been hiding yourself?" cried Berty, fondling the pony. "Don't you know I've been hunting for you everywhere and got lost, eh?"

Another neigh, and the roan rubs its cold nose up and down the little fellow's shoulder.

"Ah, none of that, you old Greasehorn, I've had some trouble to find you; but 'better late than never,' as dad says. Now won't they be pleased to see me? and sha'n't I be glad to see them?"

Vaulting on the back of the pony, the pair jog along the wheel track towards the station. Turning a bend in the track, boy and pony come in view of a party of men, tired to death, and who have been out hunting for the lost one.

A loud, glad shout of recognition, and the next moment poor little Berty is in the strong arms of his father, whose voice is husky with emotion as he mutters a prayer of thankfulness intermingled with his passionate kisses.

"Where did you get to, my son?"

"Oh, a long way, mother. It was the laughing jackass who found me."

Mother and father exchange glances.

"The child has had a touch of the sun," says the latter, stroking Berty's curls.

"Where did the jackass find you, boy?"

"Under a big gum-tree such a long, long way off," responds the child, extending his arms. "Then he brought a emu—such a big fellow, with a saddle and bridle, you know—and he brought me all the way to Fir Tree Hollow."

Stephen Wake shakes his head.

"Put him to bed, wife," he says quietly; "the poor child is not himself. A good night's sleep will set him all right again."

And Berty Wake slept well. In the early morning, however, he arose and went out into the stable yard, where the laughing jackass nodded on his perch.

"Hallo! Jack the Rover," he said, saluting the bird.

The laughing jackass opened its sleepy eye and gazed meditatively at the boy for a few moments, then broke out into its hearty guffaw: "Ha-ha-ha! Ho-ho-ho!!"

# HOP-O'-MY-THUMB.

EVERY one who knew Tiny Thumbcake loved him. He was one of eleven brothers and sisters, and the smallest mite that was ever born in the land of the cornstalk.

Tiny, though very diminutive in body, was nevertheless a hardy fellow who could run and jump like a kangaroo; moreover, he possessed the gift of knowing the language of all animals and birds, and these nicknamed him "Hop-o'-my-thumb."

The Thumbcakes were poor people, and Tiny, who loved the wild bush, determined to try his fortune as a pioneer squatter. In conversation with an old wallaby, who used to pay him periodical visits, Tiny learned that there was a vast district owned by a giant aborigine named "Slubber," where no white man had ever been and which was supposed by everybody to be a dreary wilderness without river, or lake, or anything to sustain life in the way of game. Tiny Thumbcake, or as we shall call him, Hop-o'-my-thumb, was both surprised and delighted at the news imparted to him by the wallaby—namely, that the Unknown Country, ruled over by Slubber the Giant, was both beautiful and fertile, and one of the finest climates under the Southern Cross.

And so in due time, guided by the faithful wallaby, our hero came to the country of Slubber, and took up his abode in a rich and well-watered valley, beside a high mountain, and here he formed a fine station for rearing cattle and sheep. For a whole year our little man remained hard at work unmolested.

One fine summer day a scarlet and green parrot alighted near where the little squatter was at work on his orchard fence.

"Good-day, Hop-o'-my-thumb," said the bird.

"Good-day, my friend," returned the wee man, politely raising his hat and bowing. "I'm glad to see you. What can I do for you, eh?"

"Nothing at present, thank you. I was sent by King Stork to warn you that Slubber the Giant is on his way here to destroy you," answered the parrot.

Poor Hop-o'-my-thumb, though not wanting in pluck, became much disturbed at the news. "Are you quite certain of what you say?" he asked of the parrot.

"Oh, quite," rejoined the messenger decidedly. "King Stork and the giant are great friends. He heard Slubber say that he would slay you or any white riff-raff who dared to set foot in his territory, and saw him start off straightway down the mountain to carry out his threat, therefore I posted off to warn you."

"Thank you very much," said poor Hop-o'-my-thumb. "Slubber is a big, selfish wretch. I have as much right to make a home here as he has, and I mean to show him I am not at all afraid of his bullying."

"Bravo!" cried the parrot, flapping his wings in glee. "You're a lad of mettle, and I'm glad you intend to try and take the blackfellow down a peg. Do you know, he is the most vile beast living and a great liar. Don't trust him a bit. If he finds he cannot kill you with his huge waddy, or spear you unawares, he will want to parley with you, and take you on his knee, in friendly fashion. Be careful, Hop, my boy. Don't let the wretch lay a finger on you, if you can help it.".

"Thank you, I'll take every precaution," said Hop-o'-my-thumb coolly.

"We all like you very much, my dear little Hop," added the bird kindly; "what is more, we are determined to help you against Slubber if we can. Your friend Jack, the wallaby, is waiting behind yonder ridge, with some possum friends and one or two native bears, in case you need assistance. Hark! Do you hear that noise? That's the giant; he hasn't lost much time on the road. Look! Yonder he comes."

Half way down the mountain-side a gigantic blackfellow, tall as a tree, and with a great woolly head (not unlike the big ball that is hoisted at noon on the flagstaff at the Observatory), came thundering down the stony ridges in tremendous leaps and bounds, and at the same time roaring out a hoarse shout of vengeance. He was quite nude, save for a segment of covering round his middle, and he brandished aloft a monstrous waddy, which was large enough to have felled an elephant.

"Where is that insignificant rascal who has dared to enter the domain of Slubber?" cried the angry monster, striding into the valley and confronting our hero, who did not flinch in the least before his dreaded enemy.

"Now, mite, what hast thou to say ere I slay thee?" cried the giant, at the same time whirling his club round his head with a noise like thunder.

"Try it," said Hop-o'-my-thumb, keenly watching every movement of his adversary.

"Insolent atom, take that," and Slubber aimed a blow at the little fellow, which if it had taken effect would have crushed our hero into a pulp; but Hop-o'-my-thumb nimbly avoided the giant's bludgeon, and getting between the monster's legs,

"'THOU ART VERY STRONG FOR SO SMALL A MAN.'"

gave him a cut with a sharp adze he had been using, which made Slubber roar with pain. It might have gone hard with the brave wee squatter at this moment, for the giant, reaching down, was about to clutch his small assailant, when the parrot came to the rescue. He flew full butt against Slubber's face and nearly blinded him, and Hop-o'-my-thumb, taking full advantage of the bird's help, gave his ugly foe such a slashing about his legs that the giant fell broadcast on his back, which made the ground tremble like an earthquake.

Seeing the unexpected and stout resistance made by our little hero, Slubber the Giant was fain to call a parley.

"Thou art very strong for so small a man," cried he ruefully, and at the same time rubbing his smarting shins. "What sayest thou, wilt thou do me a service? And in return thou and thine shall have this valley of sweet waters for thy pains, to do with it what ye will."

"What is the service you want to be performed?" said Hop-o'-my-thumb.

"Come nearer, and I will tell thee."

"No, not an inch," cried the little fellow stoutly. "You are near enough, my friend. Tell me what I am to do. I can hear you."

"Oh, very well," responded Slubber sullenly. "Know, then, that I have a wife."

"I wish I had one," interrupted Hop-o'-my-thumb."

"Thou shalt have mine with pleasure," retorted the giant quickly.

The little squatter laughed. "Nay," he said, "it is against the law to take anything belonging to another. Well, you were saying you have a wife."

"True, I have a wife and, I may add, one of the most inquisitive of her sex," added the giant in quite a humble tone, which contrasted strangely with his previous bombast. "Know, then, O mite, King Stork propounded three riddles to my wife, each one full of mystery, and my life is plagued out of me day and night by her to find an answer to these problems. Now, if thou canst find the secret of these things the land is thine for all time."

"What are the riddles?" inquired Hop-o'-my thumb.

The giant reflected a moment and then replied,—

"The first is: What is the most wonderful animal in the world? Second: What shoemaker makes shoes without leather, but uses instead earth, water, air, and fire, and where each of his customers wears two pairs at a time? Third: What is seen in the sky, also in the water, and sometimes on men's breasts which, being reversed, is the name for the very worst kind of vermin? Come now, O thou bull ant, canst thou explain these enigmas?"

Poor Hop-o'-my-thumb seemed dismayed for

a moment. He wanted to conciliate the giant, but how was he to frame a reply to these three difficult questions? In the midst of his cogitations he bethought him of his friend the wallaby.

"If Slubber will give me a little time, I believe I can answer the questions," said the little man with confidence. The giant assented readily.

Hop-o'-my-thumb, guided by the parrot, sought out the old wallaby, to whom he confided his trouble.

"Nothing easier, my boy," said the animal, stroking his head with his paw. "A word in your ear. These riddles are the secrets of our King and must not be made known to every one."

Then the old wallaby whispered what Hop-o'-my-thumb wanted to know, and the latter, smiling, went back to the giant Slubber.

"Well, hast thou the answers, mite?" he said.

"Oh yes," replied our hero cautiously, "but how am I to know you will keep your word with me?"

The giant laughed. Then he lay full length upon the sward, and plucking a long hair from his beard laid it across his nose. "Will *that* condition satisfy you?" he said in a rage, for Slubber knew he dare not break *that* form of oath.

"Then," said Hop-o'-my-thumb, "the most wonderful animal in the world is a pig; for it is first killed and then cured."

"Good!" cried Slubber.

"The next," continued Hop-o'-my thumb, "is— What shoemaker makes shoes without leather? Why, a horseshoer, for he uses earth, air, water, fire, in shaping his wares, and each of his customers wears two pairs."

"Bravo! Let me embrace you," entreated the giant.

"No you don't," responded the little man, with a grin. "Now for your third question. What is seen in the sky, the water, and sometimes on men's breasts? A star, of course. Reverse the spelling of star and it is rats. Are you satisfied?"

And Slubber, the black giant, wended his way home over the mountain again, a wiser man; and ever after Hop-o'-my-thumb lived in peace.

# A MAGIC WHISTLE.

HERE are low green hills and sharply outlined ridges strewn with great white blocks of quartz, gleaming in the morning sunlight. Adown the long eastern slope for miles there is a vista of park-like forest, where the wallaroo and kangaroo leap and gambol on the greensward; where green and gold parrots chatter and scream; where wild bees are humming to the morn, and where the eagle soars calm and peerless in the sapphire firmament.

One solitary figure dots this glorious landscape—a handsome, well-formed boy, with a swag upon his back, tramping slowly along the narrow track like unto one who would fain rest and eat. There is not the sign of any habitation in view; nothing but the matchless sunshine and the hills and valleys gleaming beneath in one great halo of golden glory.

Towards evening our traveller, emerging upon a lonely glade, threw off his swag and cast himself upon the soft sward and so fell asleep. When he awoke it was night, the dark blue canopy overhead was ablaze with stars. Looking round he was greatly astonished to observe the space before him aglow with a soft, subdued light, which was neither from the sun, the moon, nor the stars, but was produced by countless glow-worms and fire-flies combined, and who had formed broad festoons from tree to tree and so lit up the dell by enchantment.

Damper—for so was the wayfarer named, on account of his fondness for that Australian made cake—rubbed his eyes in great surprise, and also gave himself one or two severe punches to make certain that he was awake. The poor lad was without father or mother, and had tramped about the bush since he could walk, doing odd jobs for cockatoos (small farmers) and such-like; but a sight like this had never met his view before. His first impulse was to call out, but his voice refused its office; for at that moment he beheld a troop of black mites, no larger than his finger, march from out the gloom beyond into the radius of the light. They were all sheathed in mail armour and came onward with quick and regular step, four a-breast, their shields and spears flashing and sparkling like so many rare jewels in the sun.

They ranged themselves in regular order, shoulder to shoulder, on one side of the dell.

Then there came a second squad, equally tiny in stature, but bravely attired in cloth of gold, with miniature swords clashing and banners waving; and these formed up on the sward, opposite the first troop.

And lo! as Damper gazed in consternation, there appeared a third group; white people these, not so tall as a lady's thimble, without weapons, and robed in the most quaint fashions imaginable: some were clad in gossamer from head to heel; many had cloaks spun from wild bees' wings; others were donned in all the gaudy colours of the dragon fly; and one and all of them appeared dancing mad.

Now here, now there; in and out; up and down; in whirling mazes, they moved like the sun flashes on some bright instrument, and too quick sometimes for the eye to follow their evolutions. It was altogether a fantastic scene, and one that the eye of mortal man is rarely permitted to look upon.

For some time poor Damper was beside himself with fear. Fortunately he remained very still and quiet, and was enabled to see everything that took place, without the elves being in the least degree aware of the mortal's close proximity.

The antic gambols were so strange and grotesque that Damper had no definite idea how long they continued, or who piped the music for the occasion. One thing was clear to him, however, that the whole scene vanished as suddenly as it appeared, leaving only two of the fairy assembly, who without more ado came and perched themselves upon Damper's swag, and began a conversation. This pair, it was evident, were the King and Queen of Elfland, who, after discussing several affairs of State, spoke of a magic whistle, hidden away among the roots of a certain tree in the dell.

Damper, although he understood and could hear every word uttered by their Majesties, paid little heed to what they said until the topic of the whistle began. Then he listened greedily. He soon learned that whoever had possession of this simple instrument held the wand of a magician over animal, bird, or man, and that if he pleased to pipe, man, bird, or animal within its sound must needs dance.

The hiding-place of this wonderful instrument was very minutely described by the King, so that when the royal pair had taken their departure, Damper determined to become possessed of it. When day broke our hero arose and began his search. He had no difficulty in finding the tree, and he soon found the whistle. It was a stout reed, about six inches long, with a mouthpiece of pure gold.

Numbers of birds, from the wren to a stork, were about and around, singing their morning song. To test the efficacy of his prize, Damper placed the whistle to his mouth and began to play. The effect was indeed wonderful. Not a bird but suddenly ceased its song and began to hop and dance about in the most absurd and comical manner, that our hero had to cease playing in order to laugh.

"Oh! I think you will just be of some service to me," he said, putting the whistle in his pocket. Then he shouldered his swag and continued his journey.

He had not proceeded far when there approached from the opposite direction a very fat woman in a covered van with her husband, who was a very little man. He was on foot, driving the horse. The woman seemed in a bad temper, and was abusing her companion soundly.

Damper stopped the cart and asked the dame for a little food. "Go on with you for an idle vagabond!" she cried, shaking her huge fist at the boy. "There are far too many of your sort about the country already. I only wish we were near a township so that I might have the pleasure of sending you to the lock-up, you loafing rascal."

Such uncalled-for abuse roused Damper's ire. Without uttering a word in reply he took out his whistle and began to blow. Instantly the fat dame leapt from the trap into the road and began whirling round and round with all her might, and anon throwing herself into such ridiculous postures that the little man, her husband, and even the horse began to laugh; but their laugh was of short duration, for they also were drawn into the dance, and the pony being securely harnessed upset the conveyance and scattered its contents all over the sward.

In the meantime the unfortunate woman, puffing and blowing like a grampus, cut some very extraordinary capers under the irresistible spell of the whistle. What seemed to be part of a wild Highland reel merged into the antics of a sort of Maori war-dance, and it was wonderful to note the agility displayed by so stout a person.

The piper himself felt too indignant to laugh, otherwise the good dame's gambols would have been of brief duration. Not before all the breath had been jolted out of her anatomy did she plead for parley. Then in gasps she called out to him to "stop for mercy's sake, and she would give him all the tucker in the cart."

Our hero was by no means a bad-hearted fellow. When he saw the woman had been punished for her very rude behaviour he put the whistle aside, and assisted to raise the pony and restore the goods to the trap. Afterwards they dined together and parted on friendly terms.

Arriving late that night at a farmhouse on the billabong, Damper craved a night's shelter, which was given him. In the morning he asked for work.

"What can you do?" said the farmer.

"Oh, anything almost. I can make you dance," answered Damper.

"Yes. And, by George, you'll find I'll make you *dance*, my lad, if you talk to me like that!" retorted the farmer angrily; and so poor Damper was compelled to hump his swag farther afield.

The weather was fine, however, and the lad's heart light; so he went singing along the bush track, until he was suddenly brought to a standstill by a gruff command, "To bail up!" Right across the track he saw a big, bearded bushranger, splendidly mounted, who, seeing he was but a youth, put back his revolvers and dismounted.

Before the ruffian could approach him, however, Damper pulled out his whistle and began to play. Instantly the man and horse began their capers with one accord, and it was not until the robber had fallen exhausted on the track that our hero ceased whistling.

"I pray thee put by that dreadful thing," said the panting outlaw, "and I will fill thy pouch with gold."

"Not a bit of it," said Damper resolutely; "my terms are that you hand over to me every item of your ill-gotten treasure, horse included, else you shall dance for it, my honey."

The robber commencing to curse and swear, Damper placed the whistle to his mouth again.

"Stop! Stop! I yield to thy terms, boy," cried the other imploringly.

"Very well. Hand over your revolver. Now that belt round your waist. Now take off your boots and depart in double-quick time."

The bushranger did not need to be told twice. He fled away into the bush and was lost to sight in a moment.

Damper found the robber's belt filled with gold. He mounted the horse and rode away. And no lad in the whole continent was happier than he was that day.

# "COCKY."

## CHAPTER I.

### THE MAGIC HUT.

AN outcast in a great city. Half-clad, half-starved, kicked and cuffed, and sworn at, as if he were no better than a mongrel cur, wretched Jack Cochrane felt that he was a useless unit in the world.

Jack was a foundling, God help him! First one and then another had taken him in hand, to rear him in the way he should go and make a decent member of society of him; but the charitable intentions of his godfathers and godmothers had evidently failed, for here he stood on this cold winter's night, a full-grown youth, utterly unlettered, shivering in the keen wind, like a puppy in a wet sack.

To most of the young ragamuffins of his class he was known by the nickname of "Cocky," and while he stood beneath a lamp-post, thinking how nice and comfortable it would be to tumble into a warm bed, half a dozen city waifs like himself came roystering by.

"Hello, Cocky! Where'r you going to doss to-night? Biler, or gas-pipe? Don't you go on the wharf—there's two coppers waitin' there. Wouldn't a saveloy hot or a tater go down slick, eh? So-long! Cocky, old man!" and the squad of shoeless young vagabonds went laughing on their way.

"I must try and get in and have a snooze somewhere," muttered the lad, blowing on his finger-tips to warm them. "There's the railway—I wonder if I could find a truck with a tarpaulin on it? I will try."

The idea is acted on at once. Cocky soon finds a line of trucks covered well from the weather, into one of which he quietly creeps, and finding it snug and warm is soon fast asleep.

When he awakes it is daylight, and the sun is shining; peeping out from his cover, Cocky discovers he is far away from the city. He has been an unbooked passenger by a goods train which has travelled all night and carried him while he slept into the heart of the country.

Luckily, the train happens to be stationary at a lonely bush siding, and Cocky makes his way out of the truck and away into the scrub without being discovered. Hurrying away from the direction of the railway siding, Cocky finds himself near sundown on a narrow pathway leading over a range of high hills into a deep valley without trees, and where stands a solitary hut. An old man, much bent in form, and whose hair and beard looked as if they had not been shorn since he was born, stood at the door and gazed at our hero very curiously.

"Please could you give me a morsel to eat?" said poor Cocky, halting, faint and tired.

"Hum! You had better go farther if you fare worse," answered the old man.

"I can't go any farther," said the boy. "I'm done up completely. Pray let me stay here to-night," he pleaded.

"Hum! Rum-fuddle-em-fee! Very well. What can you do?" questioned the old fellow, his eyes glinting and glowering upon poor Cocky in a most remarkable manner, like a cat's eyes seen in the dark.

"Do?" repeated the lad boldly. "Oh, I'll do anything if you will give me some food and find me somewhere to sleep."

"Bunkum Geezer," muttered the toothless old fellow in reply. "You shall have all you want, but you must do my bidding; otherwise you shall not leave this valley alive. Do you hear?"

Cocky was desperate with all a lad's gnawing hunger, so he answered, "All right. Trot out the tucker."

Close by the hut stood a magnificent fir-tree, whose branches formed a canopy impervious to dew or rain. Beneath it stood a table already spread with dainty food. With a wave of his hand the old man pointed this out to Cocky, and said,—

"Go, eat. Your couch will be beneath the tree also. When you have eaten, sleep well, for to-morrow you will have to work—to work hard, boy." Saying which, he went into the hut and closed the door.

The famishing lad did not need a second invitation to dine. He found a stool by the table and sat down and began his dinner. There were many joints and dishes which the waif had never seen before, but they were very nice. In the midst of his repast a fine-looking magpie came fluttering down from the tree, and perching on one end of the table, eyed our hero inquisitively.

"Hallo! Who are you?" said the boy.

"Never you mind, Jack Cochrane. Can I have something to eat?"

"Of course you can," answered the lad, after his first start of surprise. "What'll you have? Here's baked snails, stewed kangaroo, fried wallaby, native companion on toast, with a lot of other things."

But the magpie without more ado perched himself upon a huge rabbit pie and began to help himself to its contents.

"Here, I say, old fellow, how do you know my name?" said Cocky, after a long pause, in which he had been staring wonderingly at the strange bird.

"I know most things," replied the magpie, whetting his beak on the table-cloth, preparatory to an attack on another dish. "I know that you have got into a very dangerous place, and that if you do not get counsel and help you will assuredly lose your life."

"That's pleasant. But who will kill me?" said Cocky, laughing.

"The old man. He's a terrible magician, Jack. It would have been better for you not to have come here."

"That's just what the old rascal said himself. But why can't I go when I like? He's in the hut, fast asleep by this time."

"No. Don't attempt to run away, Jack," said

the magpie gravely. "Old Gruff would be certain to know and would trap you like a fox before you were out of the valley. You have been kind in sharing your dinner with me and I will help you, Jack. Kindness goes a long way with us. We never forget those who have once befriended us, Cocky Cochrane."

"Who are you, then?" inquired the boy, with mouth agape in wonder.

"Your good fairy, Jack, from this moment henceforth," responded the bird in a kindly tone. "Please don't bother me with questions now, for I must be gone. Gruff is a wicked monster. He will set you to do what will seem impossible; but accept the task boldly and with cheerfulness. I will be near to help you. Now go to sleep. Goodnight."

Cocky slept soundly. In the early morning he was awakened by a loud roaring; opening his eyes, he saw standing over him a huge fellow of colossal proportions, who commanded him to arise in a voice like the rumbling noise of an express train.

"I am King Red Gum," said the monster, at the same time twirling a sapling round and round in his hand for pastime. "In yonder paddock you will find a young colt who has never been touched by the hand of man. Catch him and bring him here before I have eaten my breakfast, or I will string thee up by the heels and roast thee like a rabbit. Dost hear?"

Cocky laughed and bounded away on his errand. He found the colt, but soon discovered that it was quite impossible to approach the vicious brute without being eaten or kicked to death. He had serious thoughts of running away, when the magpie alighted near him, to whom he communicated his trouble.

"Shout *Stra fonatsa* as loudly as you can," said the bird.

"Stra fonatsa! Come here!" The wild horse pricked his ears and immediately came over to where our hero stood. He was as gentle as a lamb and suffered Cocky to lead him by the mane to where King Red Gum was waiting with his bludgeon.

"Ho! Ho! thou insignificant mortal," he cried, "so thou hast brought *Stra fonatsa*. It is well. Now I must be off for my morning gallop. Gruff! Gruff! thou lazy skunk, where art thou?"

"Here am I, master," answered the old man, appearing at the door of his hut.

"Give this ant his breakfast so that he may be ready to do my bidding when I return;" and

King Red Gum mounted his steed and rode away. Once more the old man of the hut invited Cocky to a well-furnished table, then retired within his domicile and shut the door. In the midst of his breakfast our hero was joined by the magpie, whom he welcomed cordially. He placed the choicest tit-bits before it.

"I am glad you have a kind heart, Jack, and that you are grateful for my help," said the bird, after the meal was over. "Learn, boy, I am not what I seem. None of us are, mortals or fairies."

"Who are you, please?" said Cocky coaxingly.

"I am an elfin, Jack; just that. In this country every one of us has been made the guardian or custodian of some one who has been wronged. I am the guardian of a beautiful young lady who has been stolen from her home and shut up in a spacious mansion underground. I have been awaiting your coming a long time, Cocky Cochrane, for you and you only can release my darling Brown Eyes from the thraldom of King Red Gum and his henchman, Old Gruff."

"Why did they shut up little Brown Eyes underground? What has she done?" said Cocky.

"That ugly wretch, King Red Gum, wanted Brown Eyes to marry him, and she would not.

So he turned the poor dear into a blue wren and placed her in a cage below the earth," answered the magpie in a trembling voice. "Now, Jack, we all need help from one another. If you'll help me, I'll stand by you."

"Agreed," cried the young fellow resolutely. "You have done me good service already; therefore whatever you order I am ready to obey."

"Thank you, Jack. Good-bye for the present. I can hear King Red Gum returning from his gallop."

## CHAPTER II.

### BROWN EYES.

OUR friend Cocky was not given very much time to digest his breakfast. Dismounting from his steed the giant beckoned him forward, and thus addressed him: "You lazy imp! It would suit you very well to do nothing but eat my victuals and take a sleep afterwards, but you shall work. Listen! On the other side of yon mountain there is a wide lagoon fringed with reeds and rushes. There lives the Australian wonder, a Bunyip. You must find him and ask of him three questions —the answers to which you must bring to me before sundown, otherwise your miserable life shall answer for it."

"Oh, that's quite easy," replied Cocky, with a dash of his city assurance. "I thought you were going to set me something very difficult. What are the three questions?"

"Why the leaves on the trees grow edgeways to the sun?" said the giant. "Next: What is the reason there is no water in Phantom Hollow? And last but not least: Why figs do not grow on the tree by the hut? Now begone! and bring me the answers before sundown," cried the Red Giant in a towering rage.

Our hero departed with a great show of bravado, but when he came near the lagoon his assumed swagger quickly evaporated. He had heard there was such a creature as a Bunyip, but he had never met anybody who had seen one. "Never despair," however, was Cocky's motto. He would try and find it, for the sake of Brown Eyes. He wandered about and searched in every likely place amongst the rushes, and waded in the water calling for the Bunyip. But there was no response to his call, and the sun began dipping westward.

Hereupon the magpie came upon the scene. "Hello, Jack! Looking for the Bunyip?" he cried.

"I can't find him. I don't believe there is such an animal," cried Cocky.

"Oh yes, there is; but he's neither animal nor fish, Jack—yet a mixture of both. All you have to do is to cut a reed like a whistle, slit it down the middle, then blow upon it twice."

Cocky obeyed the directions of the bird, and immediately there came forth from the middle of

"ITS EYES WERE DREADFUL TO BEHOLD, AS IT CAME SLOWLY OUT OF THE WATER."

the lake a huge monster, with a head shaped like that of a calf, and a body as large and unwieldy as a young hippopotamus. Its eyes were dreadful to behold, as it came slowly out of the water and crouched abjectly at the feet of our hero.

"What want you with me?" it cried presently.

"Tell me why the leaves of the gum-trees grow edgeways to the sun," said Cocky.

"Because it is the nature of the tree to grow its leaves edgewise, thou fool," replied the monster.

"What is the reason there is no water in Phantom Hollow?"

The Bunyip chuckled. "Because the sun has dried it up," he cried contemptuously. "What more?"

"Why do figs not grow upon the tree by the hut in King Red Gum's dell?"

"Because King Red Gum is an ass, who cannot discern a wild pine from a fig-tree. Now depart, or I shall drag thee down into the depths of the lagoon."

"Ask for a hair from his tail," whispered the magpie quickly.

"Please give me a hair from your tail," said Cocky; and ere the monster could grant or refuse the request our hero, by a sudden dexterous movement, had possessed himself of the coveted prize and was speeding away up the mountain-side like a deer, with the clever magpie flying low at his side.

"Now, Jack," cried the bird, "we must not part again until we have accomplished the release of my lady-bird Brown Eyes. Hold fast to that hair of the Bunyip's tail, for it will prove one of the most powerful weapons in the art of magic. It is a talisman to swear by, and none can resist it, as you will presently discover."

Then the magpie added a short whisper into Cocky's ear, and they descended into the dell, where the giant and Old Gruff stood awaiting our hero.

"Tiny mortal, hast thou done thy task? What are the answers?" roared Red Gum menacingly.

"By the hair of the Bunyip's tail, I command thy obedience," cried our hero sternly.

Red Gum let fall his huge waddy from his hand. With a loud cry he sank down at our hero's feet cringingly at the potent words. "Thou art the master! I am thy slave!" he cried in a submissive tone. "What wilt thou, mortal?"

"I have conquered, by jingo! henceforth thou shalt be a dingo."

Cocky had barely uttered the charm ere the huge bulk of the giant faded beneath his eyes and assumed the form of a wild bush dog. At the same moment the old man of the hut rushed to the assistance of his fallen chief; but our hero held the key, or rather the hair, of the position, and bade him stand.

"Dog shalt thou be for thy folly. I will change thee to a collie!" cried Cocky.

Immediately the fated words passed the youth's lips the old fellow was transformed into a big sheep dog, who, seeing the dingo at hand, sprang upon him at once, and while a battle royal raged between the two our hero mounted Stra fonatsa, and galloped away in company with the magpie, much farther than I could tell you in this little story.

When it was near sundown they came to a great cave, situated on a very high hill, and the magpie without more ado led our hero downward by a series of stairs cut in the solid rock, through arches and corridors, onward to an open vista of glorious country, glowing and shimmering beneath a strange but powerful light, which revealed the most minute object within their vision.

In the distance appeared a fine mansion, with a high tower in the centre of it; and when they came to the gate, they found a regiment of dwarfs on guard, who as soon as they saw the hair from the Bunyip's tail fell down on their faces before our hero and besought him to enter.

The magnificence displayed within the building was something to be remembered. Here were arches of polished marble, priceless statues, tables and couches of antique workmanship, with rich carpets woven in no mortal loom, and where everything was gleaming with velvet and thick silks and pure gold.

Wandering on in this wonderful place the magpie led Jack Cochrane to a small apartment overlooking a lovely prospect of forest scenery, dotted with lakes, glinting under the soft light. In one corner of this room was hung a golden cage containing a wee wren. This bird became very lively when it saw the magpie, and the latter was no less agitated on seeing the little wren.

"Give me the hair of the Bunyip," cried the magpie in an altered tone that Cocky hardly recognised. However, he obeyed. In an instant the room was plunged in profound darkness, while at the same moment came a musical voice, who in a loud tone cried, "Come forth, Brown Eyes! come forth from thy thraldom! Night hath fled. Behold the day!"

Then more swift and sudden than a lightning flash Cocky, the city waif, who had but winked his eyes in the darkness, opened them upon broad daylight, with the sun streaming into a magnificent apartment and upon a beautiful young lady with wonderful brown eyes, and also upon a tall, handsome young man by her side.

"Am I dreaming?" said poor Cocky, rubbing his eyes and staring at his companions.

"Not a bit of it, Jack Cochrane," said the handsome youth, smiling down upon Brown Eyes beside him. "I am your friend still, but a magpie no longer. The scene has changed, boy, thanks to your courage and steadfastness. The wren and the magpie are *Sir Plum Dough* and his affianced bride, Brown Eyes Wattle Blossom. This is our domain. It is called *The Gloaming*. Stay here with us and be our henchman."

RING DOWN THE CURTAIN.

www.ingramcontent.com/pod-product-compliance
Lightning Source LLC
Chambersburg PA
CBHW020322240426
43673CB00039B/887